Crafting White Paper 2.0

Jonathan Kantor

Crafting White Paper 2.0

Designing Information For Today's Time- and Attention-Challenged Business Reader

LuLu Publishing

Printed in the United States of America

ISBN 978-0-557-16324-3

This book is dedicated to my father, Maxwell H. Kantor, who passed away on April 10, 2008, at ninety-one years of age.

I attribute my entrepreneurial spirit to my father. He set a personal example for me during my youth that working for someone else was not an acceptable long-term strategy for happiness and longevity. After toiling for several manufacturing businesses, my father started his own company in 1965 shortly after turning 50. I was approximately the same age when I started my own company. Whether this is an inherent part of our family DNA structure, I cannot say.

What I can say is that if he were alive today, he would have appreciated my efforts to produce and publish this book. I only wish he were alive today to see it become reality. I'm sure that he is smiling down on me right now.

Contents

Acknowledgments

The creation of this book would not have been possible without the help, support, guilt, cajoling, and occasional swift kick in the behind from several important people in my life.

First, I would like to thank one of my best friends over the past twenty-six years, Paul Barker, the principal with the Afterburner Consulting Group. Paul has been a friend, mentor, guide, and manager throughout many chapters of my adult life. Paul's support in my career as a technical communications manager at J.D. Edwards Enterprise Software in Denver, Colorado, provided my first exposure to the white paper medium and its potential to influence business decision makers. Without that opportunity, I'd still be floundering behind a corporate cubicle mimicking the career path of a modern-day Dilbert.

I would also like to thank my friend Mike Stelzner of Stelzner Consulting, who has provided guidance and cooperation during the past several years in the area of white paper and social media marketing.

My reason for being is my daughter, Natalie, who is the light in my life. I am blessed to have such a talented, smart, hard-working, and wonderful daughter. Having her in my life creates a greater awareness of life's mysteries, greater reflections on my past, and an incentive to be my best.

I am also thankful for the support of my partner, Maureen Maybank, who is always there to provide her love and support through life's challenging moments. I would certainly not be the person I am today without her.

Finally, I would like to thank my mother, Trudy Kantor, for the love and support she has given me throughout her life. I have truly been blessed in this life to have such a loving parent as my mom.

About This Book

Today we live in a world of abbreviated information. For example, we no longer read newspaper articles; we glance at headlines or receive short text news alerts. We watch short sound bites on television rather than watch lengthy interviews. We send short Tweets via Twitter rather than long e-mail messages.

One of the reasons business executives are attracted to these short and succinct messages has to do with their amount of available time and attention. A growing list of new business responsibilities such as conference calls, meetings, travel schedules, online messages, social media interactions, and increased workloads have cut into the available time busy business executives have set aside for reading detailed information.

When it comes to reading white papers, many decision makers face a challenging conundrum. Executives know that white papers provide them with valuable information necessary to keep both their companies and their positions competitive. Unfortunately, the traditional all-text white paper, common with many business marketers, requires too much time to sift through countless pages of paragraph-centric information to uncover valuable solution-advantage messages. Due to the demands on their time, many executives will either forward these text-heavy white papers to lower-level subordinates in their organizations or pass on reading them altogether. When this occurs, the opportunity to engage key decision makers is lost.

To gain the attention of the time- and attention-challenged business reader, new formats that engage today's short attention decision makers must be incorporated into white paper content.

Once implemented, these elements become a highly effective way to draw business readers into white paper information, enabling detailed solution messages to be more easily delivered and assimilated by them.

The information in this book is based on over thirteen years of personal involvement with the white paper medium, interviewing both business marketers and—most importantly—customers on their perspectives and interactions with white paper information. This book will provide business marketers with a fresh set of ideas designed to improve the format of solution-oriented messages that engage today's busy business executives. This enables marketers to put critical information to better use, which is needed to be successful in today's highly competitive business marketplace.

Why "Crafting" versus Writing?

When we hear that someone practices a 'craft' we tend to think of him or her as a talented artisan. When we are introduced to a writer on the other hand, we tend to think of their role more as a productive task, rather than a craft. Certainly, there are fiction writers that have an inherent talent for creative writing, but in the business world, writers create materials that fall more into the category of work-related tasks, rather than creative by-products associated with a craft. In the view of many people, sculptors practice a craft while writers perform "grunt work".

This book is entitled, "Crafting White Paper 2.0" for a reason. If business writers and marketers wish to elevate their skills on par with a craft, they will have to incorporate more visually engaging elements beyond simply placing words on a blank sheet of paper. White paper writers in today's competitive business environment will need to incorporate design, graphics, illustrations, and photographic imagery that is more on par with the work of a craft artisan than a task-oriented business writer.

This book is designed to do just that. By following the suggestions advocated in this book, business writers and marketers can advance their skills that yield more visually appealing white papers and engage today's sophisticated business reader. In doing so, their productive roles will be perceived more as a craft than a basic business task.

Chapter 1: Understanding Today's White Paper Medium

What does the term *white paper* mean to you when you see it on a Web site, blog, or online article? Ask ten people what it is, and you'll probably get ten completely different answers. In fact, it wasn't that long ago that the term conjured up thoughts of men in white lab coats, jotting down lines of scientific code filled with strange symbols and jargon. At that time, when someone said they were writing a white paper, it was understood to be a document containing highly technical or scientific information reserved for a select, sophisticated audience and certainly not intended for general public consumption.

Fast-forward to the present day. Today's white paper has become a mature, widely accepted, and highly valued marketing medium used by every private and public sector from agriculture to zone planning. When any organization is ready to announce a new product campaign, solution strategy, brand repositioning, competitive analysis, or market perspective, the white paper is the marketing tool frequently called upon to convey that information to a target audience.

As evidence of the acceptance of white papers, if you had Googled the term *white paper* ten years ago, the number of listings would have been in the thousands. Today that same search yields a list of over one hundred million items!

The utilization of the modern white paper medium over the past ten years has been nothing short of phenomenal. Some recent quotes demonstrate how far the medium has evolved to become a fully mature marketing vehicle:

"White papers remain the most effective piece of marketing collateral, with 86% of respondents finding them moderately to highly influential in the purchasing decision" (Eccolo Media).

"The most important thing is to focus on ROI and focus on things that will make the company money, such as sales lead-generation programs, webinars, and white papers" (analyst Naylor Gray of Frost & Sullivan).

"93% of all IT buyers pass along up to half of the white papers that they read" (*InformationWeek*).

Why has the modern white paper experienced such widespread acceptance as a business-marketing tool? To understand this phenomenon, we have to first understand the document's past and how it has changed over time.

A Change in Perception

White papers are no longer considered a "geeky" information medium reserved for a select audience of technologists, scientists, programmers, or researchers. Today, white papers are used by a wide range of small, medium, and enterprise-sized commercial businesses and are considered to be a full-fledged and legitimate marketing communications vehicle that is on par with other more established marketing tools, such as brochures, Web sites, and print and broadcast commercials. If any organization sells or markets a business-to-business (B2B) solution, white papers are now considered a required awareness-building and lead generation tool. Just like a Web site, if a business doesn't have a white paper, it is considered a significant shortcoming in the eyes of a prospective business customer.

One of the reasons business decision makers appreciate white papers has a lot to do with its perception as an influential, fact-based medium. In a culture dominated by image, flash, glitz, buzz, perception, and external packaging, white papers provide a logical and educational approach to information delivery, something that can't be found with many communication vehicles today.

For example, a November 2008 study conducted by Eccolo Media, entitled "The 2008 B2B Technology Collateral Survey," showed that white papers were considered the most influential form of business collateral across five different categories polled in the study. Among the survey participants (67 percent of which were key decision makers and 33 percent influencers), 44 percent felt that white papers were either very or extremely influential over the previous six-month period.[1]

For marketers that are looking for ways to generate new business opportunities, the legitimacy of white papers has translated into an effective way to generate high quality leads. A survey conducted by Arbor Networks, an enterprise solution provider, determined that white papers were the most effective medium for generating leads. The vendor tracked the percent of leads that were received across all advertising media over the course of one year. The case study showed that offers made using white papers (49 percent) were almost twice as effective as the next two media implemented: banner ads (25 percent) and e-mail newsletter sponsorships (21 percent). Print ads garnered only a 1 percent lead return.[2]

So What Is a White Paper?

For history buffs, the origins of the white paper can be traced to the early twentieth century in the British parliament, where the documents provided legislators with background information prior to voting on specific pieces of legislation. The term was coined from a procedure that parliamentary clerks used to create condensed information for busy legislators. At that time, parliamentary clerks would often bypass the typical time-consuming process of printing and binding large research documents, opting instead to assemble their own concise versions of those tomes so that legislators could review the information in a shorter amount of time. Due to the haste associated with their production, these documents were often covered with blank sheets of white paper that incorporated either typewritten or hand-written titles on the cover. As their popularity grew, the cover became associated with the medium, and hence the nickname *white paper* became a permanent fixture in the world of printed communications.

Many business managers who are not familiar with the document's history or who are new to the medium frequently ask the question, "What is a white paper, and how is it different from other business documents?" Unfortunately, just like the many permutations of the medium itself, there is no single, standard definition. For the purposes of this book, we'll limit the definition of the medium to the commercial sector, where the bulk of today's demand lies and forms the basis of this book.

Today, there are several definitions for the term *white paper* that you'll find on popular resources throughout the Internet:

A listing on Wikipedia states: "White papers are almost always marketing communications documents designed to promote a specific company's solutions or products. As a marketing tool, these papers will highlight information favorable to the company authorizing or sponsoring the paper. Such white papers are often used to generate sales leads, establish thought leadership, make a business case, or educate customers."

Another well-established spokesperson on the topic of white papers is Michael Stelzner of the White Paper Source. He defines a white paper in his book, *Writing White Papers: How to Capture Readers and Keep Them Engaged*, as "a document that usually describes problems and how to solve them. The white paper is a crossbreed of an article and a brochure. It takes the objective and educational approach of an article and weaves in persuasive corporate messages typically found in brochures. It introduces a challenge and makes a strong case why a particular approach to solving the problem is preferred."

Both of these definitions are well-constructed attempts to define a very subjective marketing term. Let me add my own unique and succinct perspective. I define a white paper as "a document between six and twelve pages whose purpose is to educate, inform, and convince a reader through the accurate identification of existing problems and the presentation of beneficial solutions that solve those challenges."

There are several aspects that make the modern commercial white paper unique from other forms of business communications. These include the following:

1. A Condensed Size—Today, the length of a commercial white paper is typically between six to twelve pages, with the majority under eight pages. While early white papers were much longer, often encompassing tens if not hundreds of pages, the amount of time and attention that most of today's business executives have set aside for reading large volumes of complex information has made these large versions virtually obsolete. Marketers must realize that any white paper that is greater than twelve pages will probably not be read in its entirety given the business commitments and amount of time that today's business reader can devote to reading complex information.

2. Fact Orientation—One of the primary attractions with a white paper is its ability to provide educationally related content that leverages facts to validate claims and build reader credibility. This is a very unique approach as compared to other, more traditional business communication mediums such as brochures, advertising, Web sites, and blogs whose main purpose is to promote a company, brand, philosophy, or approach by making a connection through a visual or emotional appeal. With a white paper, any subsequent call-to-action, such as visiting a Web site or contacting the sponsor, takes place once the viability of the advocated solution has been established through the presentation of fact-based information.

3. Cross Positioning—The white paper is the only medium that occupies the middle ground between diametrically opposed sides of business communications.

On one side, there are highly technical documents, such as user manuals, technical primers, or research documents, whose primary intent is to educate by providing pure, unbiased facts. These documents present information without a personal opinion or conjecture. Most are absent visual enhancements such as layout or design that could be used to evoke an emotional appeal. Any graphics in these documents are often very simple and are used as a means of reinforcing the factual data presented in the white paper.

On the other side are highly impressionable documents such as brochures, Web sites, flash animation, digital audio and video, broadcast commercials, and interactive multimedia. The primary purpose with these mediums is to appeal to audience emotion, elicit a positive impression, and build brand affinity that will ultimately result in an additional action or response, such as contacting the sponsor or purchasing a solution.

White papers occupy the space between these two polar opposites and borrow certain attributes from both sides. From the technical side, white papers educate and inform their readers through the logical presentation of factual data and information. On the emotional side, white papers use visual enhancements such as charts, graphs, and illustrative design to build affinity and create a positive appeal whose purpose is to elicit a call to action.

4. Unique Appeal—The term *white paper* creates the perception of a premium document of highly valuable information with a unique appeal. When the label *white paper* is used on the cover of a document, it is understood that the context, format, and presentation of the information contained within it will be of a higher value than other mainstream business information sources. With this in mind, many marketers often leverage the term *white paper* as part of a product launch, new business strategy, Web site campaign, or other critical strategic initiative to attract new customers. Other mainstream communication vehicles such as brochures, articles, annual reports, 10K statements, case studies, PR announcements, Web sites, or technical primers do not hold a similar premium image or value in the eyes of a business reader.

5. Logical Flow—A good white paper will walk a reader through the logical flow of information, starting from broad industry issues, proceeding to background information and statistics, and ending with more specific problems and business challenges associated with the topic. Once these issues have been identified, a well-written white paper will then present specific solution-oriented information that discusses how the previously identified challenges and problems can be resolved by the implementation of the advocated solution.

6. Broad Audience—The methodical flow of information equally appeals to both the uninformed and the well-informed reader alike. Using a step-by-step approach that presents background information, problem assessments, and solution advantages, any type of professional reader should be able to read a white paper and walk away with a similar level of knowledge on the topic. This unique approach, which is similar to presenting a legal case in a court of law, allows business marketers to use a single white paper to reach a broader audience for their solutions than if they had written two different documents for separate customer segments.

7. Unique Presentation—The unique manner in which both text and graphic information is applied to the presentation of business information allows the reader to fully comprehend the key issues surrounding the white paper topic. For example, most white papers will often use the following elements to aid in the information delivery process: summaries (both executive and concluding), callouts (also known as pull quotes), bullet lists, graphics (business, concept, and descriptive illustrations), tables, shaded text boxes, and a host of additional formatting options. No other business communication vehicle offers its readers such a wide variety of information formats and techniques.

8. Wider Use—There is no other single business communication medium that is as multi-faceted and has as many uses as a white paper. The development of a single white paper can be used for both online and offline marketing tactics that include a Web site lead generator, printed collateral, direct mail campaigns, e-mail marketing campaigns, tradeshow distribution, a sales call leave-behind piece, a supplement for a live or online presentation, or an attachment for a single e-mail message. By regularly updating the information contained in a white paper, the investment made in its development can continue to provide a significant return on investment year after year as marketing plans and requirements change over time.

9. Greater Measurability—In comparison to other traditional marketing mediums like print and broadcast advertising that use arbitrary measures of effectiveness such as cost-per-thousand or estimated viewership, white papers provide a more accurate measurement of effectiveness.

Because the majority of white papers are distributed online, white papers can be offered via a corporate Web site, public forum, or paid content syndication provider. It can also be "ReTweeted" (RT) or forwarded from one user to many others via social media sites such as Twitter. This enables marketers to count the number of clicks, downloads, or ReTweets (RTs), especially if a Web site landing page is referenced as a call to action in a concluding summary. White papers can also be offered via search engines, where the number of visitors that click on advertisements for the white paper can be measured and compared over time.

As a result of these unique attributes, white papers provide as much value to their marketing hosts as they do for their target business audience, a key attribute that is quite rare in today's business marketplace.

10. An Evolutionary Medium—Due to its use of the Internet as a primary means of distribution, white papers are continuously evolving to accommodate new technologies, approaches, and designs that improve reading and comprehension. As new online communication techniques become popular, white papers are often quick to incorporate them. When commercial Web sites became popular in the mid-1990s, white papers were shared online. As the Adobe Acrobat PDF file format was released, white paper marketers quickly accepted the new standard, and it became an easy way to format and distribute white papers for online viewing. When audio podcasts became popular, marketers developed audio versions of printed white papers. As social media sites have become popular, marketers are quickly moving to adopt the white paper medium as an integral part of business message delivery. This process will continue to evolve the white paper medium as new online technologies are released.

These advantages not only demonstrate the multifaceted nature of the white paper medium to influence a business audience, but it also demonstrates its longevity and durability within a changing business marketplace. Seeing how far the medium has changed since its birth at the start of the twentieth century, it will most assuredly be around for many decades into the future.

Chapter 2: The Relationship Between Time and Attention

Do you remember the old adage "time is money"? This statement is more applicable given today's economic environment than ever before.

While the term has always meant that time was valuable, it seemed that in previous generations we had more time set aside for reading information than we do today. Perhaps it was due to the fact that producing documents was a time consuming and laborious task, and as a result they appreciated them more than today, where a document can be created and printed in a fraction of the time. After all, creating a fifty-page white paper in the past required the use of paper, pencils, erasers, a typewriter, and a complex printing process to create the final product. This took a significant amount of time and effort from start to finish. Once these large documents were created, it was probably considered bad etiquette to skim through it after such a process. As a result, business executives of that era probably took more time to read each printed white paper handed to them by a manager or co-worker.

Today of course, we don't have the luxury of devoting an extensive amount of time to the reading task. Not only has time become equal to money, but given the expanding workloads of most full-time employees, time has actually become more valuable because we have a finite amount of it. Our growing list of conference calls, meetings, travel schedules, e-mails, text messages, social media updates, and new work responsibilities must now fit into the fixed time frame of a forty-hour (or perhaps more accurately, sixty-hour) workweek in today's fast-paced workplace. With more work, many executives find that there is precious little time available to perform such extracurricular activities as reading complex and detailed information like white papers.

In fact, a recent study from an industry researcher firm, Gartner, Inc., has confirmed this trend and its impact on the time executives spend reading. The study showed that C-level executives spend an average of fifteen hours per week using the Internet, eight hours watching TV, and five hours listening to the radio, but they spend only five hours reading newspapers and a mere four hours reading magazines.[3]

The primary challenge that many executives face is that the only way to maintain both their own and their employers' competitive edge is to read high quality marketing information delivered via white papers. While white papers are a great way to provide valuable business information, unfortunately many are formatted in such a way that makes it difficult for time-challenged executives to read and comprehend the information in a rapid amount of time.

For these time-constrained executives, this situation presents a problem. How does an executive devote an increasingly limited amount time (that often requires a greater amount of personal time) for reading complex, solution-oriented information? Or do they pass on the reading task due to their time constraints, knowing full well that it may mean that their organization (and often their own position) may be less secure within the competitive landscape?

Unfortunately, the traditional ten- to twenty-page white paper that represented the gold standard only a few years ago won't fit into today's time-constrained work schedule. When executives see lengthy white papers of countless pages with unstructured text, many won't even bother to read them. Even if it could be determined that a large white paper had valuable information, the demands on executive time still results in delegating the reading responsibility to a lower-level subordinate.

As the document finds its way to lower-level managers who are not responsible for the final decision-making process, the opportunity to use the white paper as a means of engaging the key decision maker is lost. Therefore the length of the document plays a role in the decision. Too short and it doesn't provide enough information to make a valid business decision. Too long and it defeats its original purpose in influencing a major business decision maker.

Therefore, business marketers must find new ways to evolve the white paper medium to appeal and influence key executive decision makers. The goal is not just a shorter white paper but also a more effective one. To understand how the white paper medium must evolve to accommodate the needs of today's readers, it is first important to understand the differences between the way that writers write white papers and the process in which readers read them.

Chapter 3: Comparing Reading and Writing Styles

There is a significant difference between the way that business writers write white papers, and they way that their intended audience reads them. Understanding this difference can provide writers with a greater appreciation of how white paper information must be formatted to be more in sync with the needs of today's business reader.

White paper writers use what is referred to as a serial approach to develop document information. In other words, the first page (usually an introduction) is written, then page 2, then page 3, etc. until the end of the white paper is reached. Unfortunately, writers that use this approach assume that readers *will* read all the information in the same order in which it was written. In other words, writers assume that readers will read page 1 in its entirety *before* they read page 2, and page 2 in its entirety *before* page 3, etc. In reality, the reading process used by today's time- and attention-challenged business reader is very different from this serial approach.

The Serial Approach To Writing Business Documents

Writers apply a serial process and expect the reader to follow it.

Instead of a serial reading method, business executives read information by using what is referred to as a layered approach. Using this process, the reader reviews the white paper several times, applying a longer period of time with each subsequent review, as long as engaging information can be uncovered with each pass. As these "rewards" are found after each "layer," the reader advances to the next reading level and devotes a greater amount of time and attention to the white paper content. This is what is commonly referred to as "drawing the reader into the content," which is shown in the illustration on the next page.

Here is an explanation of each of these review layers and how they relate to meeting the requirements with today's time-challenged business reader:

Layer 1: The Skimming Layer—When business readers first take a look at a newly downloaded white paper, they quickly skim through the entire document page by page, looking for specific pieces of information that might be of interest to them.

The Layered Approach with Today's Business Reader

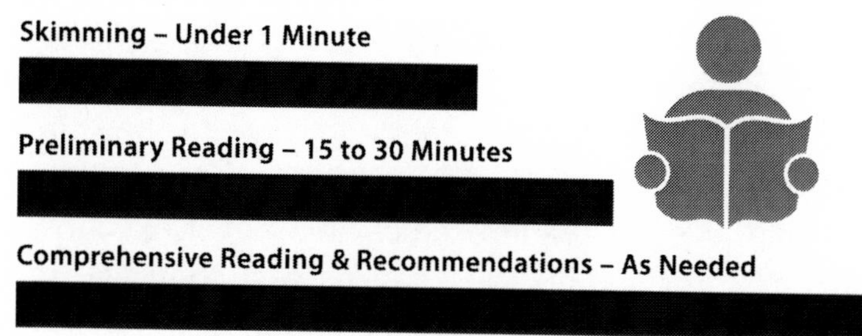

Business readers devote more time as they find valuable information.

This quick search is designed to answer two fundamental questions:

- *Will this information provide valuable answers that can solve a business problem I am experiencing?*
- *Will this white paper be a good investment of my limited and important reading time?*

During this first skim reading process, which usually takes about a minute, readers look for key elements such as business graphics, quotes, tables, illustrations, or other pieces of formatted text that will grab their attention and engage their interest in the content of the white paper. If they find one or more of these items, they will become more engaged with the content and will advance to the next reading level.

Layer 2: The Preliminary Reading Layer—Once readers have found rewarding informational elements in layer 1, they will devote an additional amount of time to understanding it. For example, if they notice a business graphic or chart, they may read the paragraphs that are placed before or after that graphic on the page. During this stage, they will often devote fifteen to thirty minutes to reading this supplemental information. If the information answers several of their key questions or seems to address current business needs, then they advance to the third and final layer.

Layer 3: The Comprehensive Reading and Recommendation Layer—Once fulfilled with valuable information in layers 1 and 2, readers advance to the third layer, where they will devote time to reading the entire white paper on a comprehensive level. If readers (such as C-level executives) are fully engaged at this point, the chances that they will read the entire white paper increase dramatically. If the reader is not engaged or has not found valuable information in layers 1 or 2, then there is a greater likelihood that they will forward the white paper to a subordinate and/or another member of the decision-making team for their input. This makes the call-to-action process with a key decision maker more difficult because they are further removed from the direct influence of the white paper.

Integrating the Reading Layers

Using a serial writing process, most white papers assume that every reader will take a comprehensive approach and read the entire paper from start to finish. To obtain the attention of today's time- and attention-challenged business readers, white paper marketers must integrate their information within all three layers using a variety of visual enhancements that will not only attract readers' attention but also provide them with an incentive to read a greater portion of the white paper. This requires gaining their attention at both the initial skimming layer and preliminary reading layers.

Unfortunately, most "all-text" white papers, which are absent visual enhancements, do not engage readers from the start, thereby making it difficult for them to move on to reading layers 2 and 3. When they are not provided with enough 'attention-generating' elements at the initial skimming layer, business readers are less likely to become engaged and more likely to become distracted by other stimuli such as office events, phone calls, or messages. Even worse, they may be turned off by such text-heavy documents and read other white papers that are more visually engaging, given their limited amount of time and attention.

To connect with today's reader, white papers must incorporate a series of new attention-generating elements at each of these three layers. This process is critical, especially at the first two layers, where readers will determine whether they will invest their time to reading the entire white paper and advancing to the third and final layer.

In many ways, white papers can take their cues from the evolution currently taking place within the online social media environment such as Twitter, which is designed to grab reader attention and quickly deliver short, quick, and succinct business messages. As users of social media messaging become more accustomed to the format and style that is part of this communications medium, their expectations and comfort level with other, more complex and more traditional marketing communication mediums will change as well.

Chapter 4: Social Media and Reader Attention Spans

It doesn't take a degree in rocket science to determine that social media is a hot topic in today's online B2B communications marketplace. In fact, this medium is growing at such an exponential rate that it's becoming difficult to accurately measure its growth. According to a white paper entitled "The Sum of Social Media—Is It All Just Hype?" from InHouse Assist LLC, from 2008 to 2009, Twitter grew an astronomical 1,382 percent to over seven million users, and Facebook grew 228 percent to over sixty-five million users.[4] (See chart below.)

The Explosive Growth of Social Media

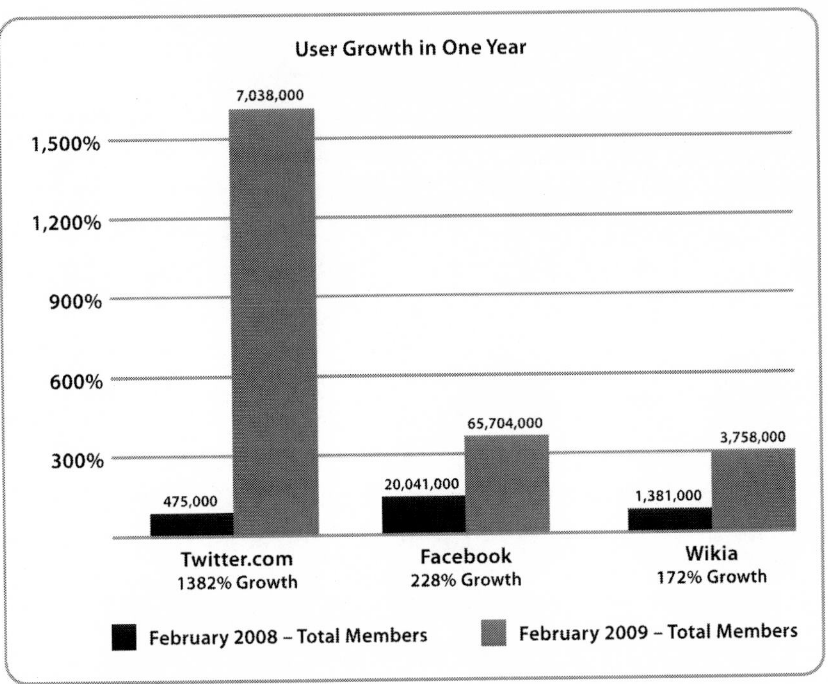

Source: InHouse Assist LLC, May 2008

Social media messaging reinforces short-attention communications.

The widespread acceptance of these communication mediums can only mean one thing: social media is here to stay. Business marketers must now accommodate social media techniques into their existing marketing programs to attract new customers and retain existing ones.

As the number of social media users grows, their expectations of business information standards are changing as well. Just as social media is best exemplified by its integration with concise, rapid, digital information (HTML pages, PDF files, video, audio, etc), traditionally formatted business information such as text-based white papers must change as well. If the white paper medium is unable to adopt and change to accommodate the rapidly changing requirements associated with a social media-savvy audience, then the effectiveness of the white paper medium will also become compromised, leading to the eventual demise of the entire medium itself.

What Is Social Media?

Social media is a new and very popular way of building online social networks with other users that share similar interests, backgrounds, or experiences through the regular update of short quick messages. Both by searching and by "following" other members that share common interests and leveraging their following in return, your network of social contacts grows. Over time this can lead to new communication groups, business opportunities, relationships, and hopefully, business leads.

The online resource Wikipedia.org defines social media in this way: "Social media is online content created by people using highly accessible and scalable publishing technologies. Social media is a shift in how people discover, read, and share news, information, and content; it's a fusion of sociology and technology, transforming monologues (one to many) into dialogues (many to many) and is the democratization of information, transforming people from content readers into publishers. Social media has become extremely popular because it allows people to connect in the online world to form relationships for personal, political, and business use."[5]

Social Media and Short Attention Spans

One of the reasons that social media such as Twitter and Facebook have become so popular is the various forms of communications that have been applied that appeal to users with a limited amount of time and attention. These environments feature photos captured from digital cameras, short statements from connected users, or segments captured from the popular video-sharing site YouTube.com. In Twitter, a social media site characterized by sending out messages of no more than 140 characters, a user can scan thousands of these short messages, select the ones that are important to them, and immediately go to an attached hyperlink representing a corresponding Web site or document. There the user can download supplemental information such a white paper or other Acrobat PDF/Word document to obtain further information related to that short message.

Twitter: A Popular Social Media Environment

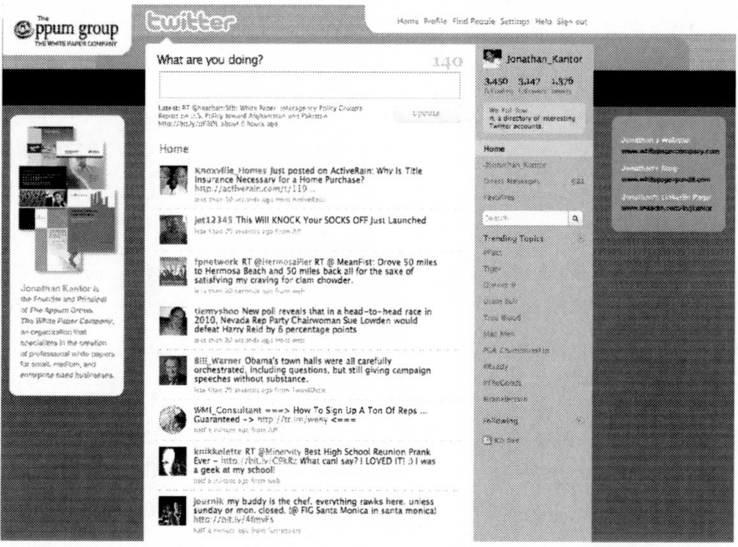

Twitter uses short, quick messages of 140 characters or less.

One of the reasons for the popularity of social media is the layered approach to accessing information, which is similar to the way that a skim reader reviews and reads a white paper, flipping quickly through it upon initial exposure to the document. With social media, users can scan a wide variety of topics or issues, create a subset of filtered topics of interest, and drill down to find a specific piece of information that accommodates their specific business needs within a short timeframe.

As social media environments such as Facebook, Twitter, LinkedIn, YouTube, and blogs become more popular, this unique short-messaging style will become a standard that users will apply to assimilating large amounts of complex business communications, such as white papers.

For example, rather than reading each page of a document in its entirety from beginning to end, short attention oriented readers will seek out specific pieces of information such as a sidebar callout, a business graphic, or a portion of an abstract summary before they proceed to reading more lengthy or detailed information. Based on how well that brief piece of information addresses their specific needs at that moment, readers will either be compelled to read an additional amount of detailed information or disengage from the reading process altogether. In all likelihood, given today's short attention spans, most readers will not have the patience to read large volumes of lengthy text content without first reading information in a shorter form such as an abstract summary, a list of bulleted text, text encased in a shaded box, or a graphic illustration.

The relationship between social media and white papers is the classic left brain/right brain comparison. The creative (left) side of social media grabs our attention using a graphic symbol, video, illustration, or picture, while the logical (right) side of social media is fulfilled with detailed information such as facts, statistics, references, and data. In this same way, white papers must now appeal to both sides of a reader's brain. While most white papers fulfill the right (logical) side, many still need to incorporate attributes representing the left (creative) side to further engage the social media oriented, short attention reader to the content.

This concept is one of the key foundational points behind what is referred to as a "White Paper 2.0" strategy. Using this strategy, attention-challenged readers are provided with a variety of formats, visual elements, and techniques that allow them to quickly determine the following:

1. If the white paper solution can be used to address their unique business problem(s).

2. Based on the quality of that content, if the white paper is worth the investment of their valuable time.

3. If the presentation of information in that white paper can be read in a way that best accommodates the limited amount of time and attention they can devote to reading complex information.

Chapter 5: How Much Information Is Enough?

Designing information for the short attention reader has become increasingly important, but does that mean your white paper has to be reduced to a single page of short lines? At some point, white papers must provide "meat on the bones" and give their readers a certain amount of valuable, educational content. The question given today's short attention reading spans is this: how much content in a white paper is enough, and how much is too much for a reader to assimilate in one reading?

An article on this topic from author Jakob Nielsen, entitled "Long vs. Short Articles as a Content Strategy," provides some valuable insight related to the way that readers read online articles that can be applied to the white paper medium.[6] With this data, marketers can calculate the most appropriate size and costs associated with their content that will generate the best possible results.

One important concept that the article uses to determine an appropriate content size is a cost/benefit metric for reading, which has two components:

1. Cost—Calculated as the total amount of time needed to read an article or Web site (or in this case, a white paper).

2. Benefit—Calculated as the extent to which users obtain some valuable idea (such as how to lower costs or generate greater profitability or productivity) as a result of spending their time reading that content.

An important point in this study was that as online content becomes longer, readers became more distracted and searched for other information. Hence, the benefit to the reader decreased as the article became longer. According to Nielsen:

"When the user stops reading one article, starts searching for something else to read, and starts reading the next article, no benefit is gained during the user's search time. (Search in this example indicates any user activity aimed at finding the next interesting article, whether it's using a search engine, a site's navigation system, or any other method of finding the next thing to read.)

"The data clearly showed that users gained greater benefits from sticking to a diet of short articles. People want to skim highlights."

Nielsen's findings back up a key principle behind short attention marketing, specifically that the longer the white paper, the greater the chance that the reader will become distracted by a host of other stimuli, including phone calls, e-mail messages, meetings, or personal conversations.

But shorter doesn't necessary mean better in this case. If it did, we would see a plethora of one-page white papers abound. When a white paper gets too short, especially less than five pages, the content that can accommodate that minute size is exclusively focused on a solution and its attributes.

According to a 2009 study conducted by the InformationWeek Business Technology Network, over five hundred professional information technology (IT) managers and buyers were asked about the "right" length of a white paper. Approximately 86 percent of these executives wanted white papers under ten pages, with 50 percent wanting even shorter sizes, such as under five pages.[7]

What we can learn from the Nielsen and InformationWeek research studies can be applied to our White Paper 2.0 strategy to design the ideal white paper length for these short attention spans. Here are some suggestions towards this goal:

1. Minimal Length—While the temptation may be to create a one-, two-, three-, or four-page white paper as the result of the need for cost containment, the limited amount of content that will fit into these small sizes will be primarily limited to a presentation of solution attributes and advantages. While many decision makers view these short white papers as "sales documents," they also restrict the degree of affinity that can be built with the reader. A better minimum requirement for a short white paper would be five to six pages as follows:

Section Type	Ideal Length
Executive Summary	1 page
Introduction	1 page
Problem Assessment	1 page
Solution Advantage	2 page
Concluding Summary	1 page

2. Maximum Length—On the other end of the document spectrum, any white paper that exceeds ten to twelve pages is far too much for the short attention reader to assimilate in one reading session. If you find that your white paper exceeds this length (even with the addition of graphics), it might be best to break up the white paper into separate documents or review the amount of content devoted to each section. An ideal ten-page paper would look like this:

Section Type	Ideal Length
Executive Summary	1 page
Introduction	1 page
Problem Assessment	2 pages
Solution Advantages	2 pages
Case Study	1 page
Concluding Summary	1 page
About Sponsor/Contact	1 page

Rather than applying a reduced size white paper to address the dilemma of the short-attention reader, a superior strategy would be to use an executive summary at the beginning of the paper. Summaries such as these provide that reader with an abstract of highly detailed information. Such a synopsis allows busy executives to determine how much information they wish to read to assess the featured solution. A presentation on how to craft an effective executive summary for the short attention reader follows in a subsequent chapter of this book.

By applying these guidelines as part of a White Paper 2.0 strategy, you can increase the chances that your key solution messages will be seen, understood, and retained by a short attention reader.

Chapter 6: Why the Traditional White Paper Won't Work

Take a look at a traditional white paper, such as one published by a government or academic entity or a scientific researcher. Most of these groups use a traditional all-text format with one or more of the following attributes that are no longer effective with today's time- and attention-challenged executive reader:

- Large page length
- Text-oriented design
- Paragraph-centric delivery mechanisms
- A lack of summaries (executive or concluding)
- A lack of graphics

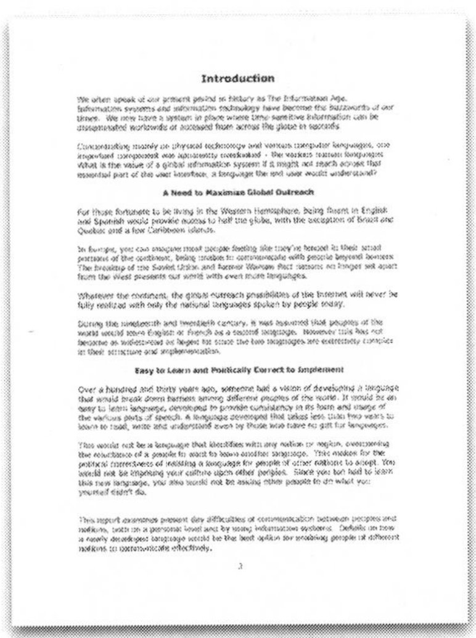

Introduction

We often speak of our present period in history as The Information Age. Information systems and information technology have become the buzzwords of our times. We now have a system in place where time-sensitive information can be disseminated worldwide or accessed from across the globe in seconds.

Concentrating mainly on physical technology and various computer languages, one important component was apparently overlooked - the world's human languages. What is the value of a global information system if it might not reach across that essential part of the user interface, a language the end user would understand?

A Need to Maximize Global Outreach

For those fortunate to be living in the Western Hemisphere, being fluent in English and Spanish would provide access to half the globe, with the exception of Brazil and Quebec and a few Caribbean islands.

In Europe, you can imagine most people feeling like they're [illegible] in their [illegible] portions of the continent, being unable to communicate with people beyond borders. The breakup of the Soviet Union and former Warsaw Pact nations no longer set apart from the West presents our world with even more languages.

Whatever the continent, the global outreach possibilities of the Internet will never be fully realized with only the national languages spoken by people today.

During the nineteenth and twentieth century, it was assumed that peoples of the world would learn English or French as a second language. However this has not become as widespread as hoped for since the two languages are extremely complex in their structure and implementation.

Easy to Learn and Politically Correct to Implement

Over a hundred and thirty years ago, someone had a vision of developing a language that would break down barriers among different peoples of the world. It would be an easy to learn language, developed to provide consistency in its form and usage of the various parts of speech. A language developed that takes less than two years to learn to read, write and understand even by those who have no gift for languages.

This would not be a language that identifies with any nation or region, overcoming the reluctance of a people to want to learn another language. This makes for the political correctness of initiating a language for people of other nations to adopt. You would not be imposing your culture upon other peoples. Since you too had to learn this new language, you also would not be asking other people to do what you yourself didn't do.

This report examines present day difficulties of communication between peoples and nations, both on a personal level and by using information systems. Details on how a newly developed language would be the best option for enabling people of different nations to communicate effectively.

3

A Large Page Length

As the white paper evolved from its origins as a government document in the 1920s, one attribute that has remained is its ability to present as much relevant data on an issue as possible. This strategy has resulted in the creation of large tomes of information, often ranging in a document length from ten to fifty pages, and on occasion, several hundred pages!

Unfortunately, given the demands on their time and attention, most executives cannot read these large documents. When confronted by a ten- to fifty-page white paper, most will quickly skim through it, send it to a subordinate in their organization, or opt out of reading it altogether.

As the responsibility to read these large white papers gets pushed down into lower levels of the organizational chart, the ability for the marketer to influence the key decision makers become more difficult.

A Text-Oriented Design

At the beginning of the twentieth century, documents were produced using analog devices such as pens, typewriters, and large printing presses that made the process of incorporating pictures or illustrations very difficult. As white papers became more popular, especially in business circles, this text-oriented format became an unwritten standard that was commonly associated with the entire white paper medium.

After many decades, even with the advent of personal computers that can easily incorporate text and graphics, most white papers continued to use an all-text format as the only means of delivering critical business information. As a result, many organizations still feel that the text-oriented design is the best format to use when producing a white paper. Unfortunately, an all-text format makes rapid reader engagement more difficult, since large portions of information must be read to uncover bottom-line solution messages. Today's time- and attention-challenged business executives simply don't have the time their previous counterparts had for this task.

A Paragraph-Centric Delivery Mechanism

As far back as the stone tablet, mankind has produced information on a line-by-line or paragraph-by-paragraph basis for every form of communication. For modern white papers, it stands to reason that this same orientation would be applied.

The problem with the paragraph-centric approach is the assumption held by the marketer that the reader *will* read each paragraph in an established order to understand the key messages in the paper. If the reader doesn't follow that specific order or skips ahead to another page, key messages that the marketer intended to be delivered to the reader may be missed.

The paragraph approach used by most traditional white papers also assumes that readers have lots of time on their hands to read each and every paragraph in a set order, starting with the first page, continuing to the second, then the third, etc., until the entire white paper is read. With the limited amount of time available for reading in today's demanding business environment, the probability that an executive decision maker will read an entire text-heavy white paper is quite low. Most will pass on the opportunity to read these documents altogether.

The Lack of Summaries (Executive or Concluding)

One of the shortcomings with most traditional white papers is their lack of either an executive or a concluding summary. This is due to several factors, including project budgets, a lack of creativity, or a false understanding of readers and their reading style.

Unfortunately, many white papers do not include summaries in their traditional text formats, or if they do, marketers fail to leverage their unique qualities in a way that will engage readers and draw them into the primary content. Many executive summaries are difficult to distinguish from formal introductions and appear to be repetitive to many readers. Concluding summaries, on the other hand, often comprise a simple ending that fails to impart key take away messages necessary for reader retention. In addition, since concluding summaries are often read first by the skim reader, many marketers who leave them out fail to engage the reader and thus never realize the opportunity to use these summary sections to make valuable first and last impressions.

The Lack of Graphics

The intellectual that first coined the phrase "A picture is worth a thousand words" was clearly ahead of his time with regard to the issue of business communications.

One glaring mistake with the traditional all-text white paper is its lack of graphic elements such as business charts, illustrations, concept graphics, or workflow diagrams. The use of an illustration in a white paper means that a business reader can quickly assimilate the point, an important advantage with a time- and attention-challenged reading audience.

On the other hand, describing that same concept using several paragraphs or a page full of text requires more time and increases the opportunity to skim through that text. It also increases the chance that a short attention reader will become distracted by other stimuli or events around them. The greater the amount of required text, the lower the probability that the reader *will* read that text, grasp essential marketing messages, and take action such as making contact or passing along that white paper with a positive recommendation.

The (Text) Bottom Line

If a white paper can't engage its readers during the initial reading and review process, those readers won't continue to read the subsequent pages and instead may be distracted by other commitments or consider other solutions that may meet their specific business needs.

While the traditional all-text white paper may still be an accepted document standard in government, academic, or scientific sectors, it no longer fits as a viable medium in an age of colorful, short, digital information commonly found in social media. As business users become accustomed to these new forms of media and communications, they will be less willing to read a text-only or text-heavy white paper.

Chapter 7: Why Is the All-Text White Paper Popular?

If you're a fan of white papers, at some point you've probably seen an all-text white paper. They are most popular with government agencies, academic, scientific, and research entities, industry analysts, and some institutional commercial businesses.

These white papers are best exemplified by their use of one single typeface or font and size throughout the entire document. The font that is often chosen for these documents typically has an administrative look. You've seen these fonts before. These fonts are often used on a variety of official forms, procedural documents, or "how-to" guides and are identified as Times Roman, Courier, Arial, Helvetica, etc. in your computer system. If traditional white papers use any special character formatting, it is very simple, such as bold, underlining, and italics. All-text white papers have an apparent absence of any color, graphics, charts, or illustrations. They also include a table of contents but are absent either an executive or concluding summary.

But why do these institutional entities believe that the all-text format is especially effective for their target audience? It's a question that begs for an answer. Could it be a lack of creativity? Perhaps it is a belief that the audience for these white papers does not require or need any graphics? Could it be a mentality of "not rocking the boat" and going with the same format that has been used by these entities over the course of several decades without change? Maybe it's an assumption that the integration of colorful design, charts, illustrations, and other graphic elements would be viewed as a "sales brochure," thereby diminishing the credibility of the white paper?

Whatever the reason may be, the authors of these documents assume that the reader has both the inclination and time to read the entire document from cover to cover in an established order to understand bottom-line solution messages. In a government environment, the target audience for these documents—namely the administrative manager—often does not have the time to read them, opting instead to have a subordinate, assistant, or administrator conduct a review summary. For example, members of Congress rarely read these documents, delegating the reading responsibility to their administrative assistants, interns, law clerks, or other support resources for subsequent review and feedback.

So if the audience for these white papers does not read them from cover to cover, the question that must be asked is why publish white papers in this format to begin with? Clearly this all-text format is diametrically opposed to the needs and requirements of the time- and attention-challenged executive.

Rather than rely on the traditional all-text format, today's white paper marketers should be considering new formatting options that will grab today's short attention reader and create an incentive for reading more detailed and valuable information.

Changing the Traditional All-Text Format

To deliver critical messages for today's business executives, a new approach is necessary. Information must now be delivered using visual elements that will grab the attention of busy executives in the limited amount of time they have set aside for reading complex information. Once they can quickly gauge whether a white paper contains the type of valuable information that they need to make current business decisions, they can allocate the appropriate amount of time necessary to read the paper in its entirety. By adding a new set of visual formatting elements, critical solution-oriented business messages can be delivered in a more effective fashion that is best suited to address the needs of these readers.

The addition of any combination of these elements is referred to as a "White Paper 2.0" strategy. While Internet communication options such as social media are becoming more important to a growing number of online business users, the traditional white paper format that used to consist of a series of pages containing nothing more than mono-font oriented left-flush paragraphs is no longer effective. This traditional format must now go the way of the typewriter and Gutenberg printing press and be left to the pages of history.

In the next several chapters, we will explore the concept of a White Paper 2.0 strategy in greater depth, along with each of the components that are contained within this strategy.

Chapter 8: What Is a White Paper 2.0 Strategy?

If you've been using the Web for some time, the term *2.0* should be familiar to you. It's been applied to many Web-oriented concepts, usually to the concept of a next-generation application of technology. The term *Web 2.0*, for example, refers to the second generation of Web development and design tools. It is characterized as facilitating communication, information sharing, interoperability, user-centered design, and collaboration. The implementation of Web 2.0 concepts have led to Web-based communities such as blogs, online forums, wikis, hosted services, podcasts, social-networking sites, document and media-sharing sites, and many others.

The term *2.0* also relates to the concept of breaking with old traditions. When the Web first became popular in the mid-90s, it wasn't much more than an electronic billboard, hosting static HTML text and GIF or JPEG pictures. In an effort to demonstrate how far Web technologies have evolved since that time, the term *Web 2.0* was coined. Now when users see the phrase *Web 2.0*, they know that the solution represents a significant advancement from its first generation counterpart.

A White Paper 2.0 strategy employs a similar concept. Just as Web technologies needed the label *2.0* as a differentiator from first generation solutions, traditional white papers also need to break from their text-oriented past and seek new dimensions to appeal to a short-attention, social media-savvy audience.

A White Paper 2.0 strategy applies several elements, such as design, color, text formatting, spacing, sizing, technologies, and orientation, to build on the legacy established by the traditional text-based white paper. While a traditional text white paper was designed with readers that had lots of time on their hands to read lengthy volumes, a White Paper 2.0 paper is designed to educate readers that have constraints on their available reading time. A White Paper 2.0 strategy is designed to use information that quickly grabs reader attention to deliver essential business messages designed for rapid comprehension and assimilation.

The Components of a White Paper 2.0 Strategy

The components of a White Paper 2.0 strategy comprise six key elements that are designed to work together to form a cohesive single unit:

- A concise size
- An online design point
- A greater use of color
- The application of layout and design
- Attention-oriented text enhancements
- Online sharing and distribution

A Concise Size

As the original white paper transitioned from that of a government document to the world of academia and finally onto the realms of science and technology, its size grew with each transition. Throughout the decades of the 1980s and 1990s, it was not uncommon to find white papers that encompassed anywhere from twenty to one hundred pages.

As white paper popularity grew in the technology sector during this period, the audience for these documents moved from that of technical professionals (MIS directors, CIOs, developers) to business professionals (C-Level, senior, and mid-level managers). Along with a changing reader, its size also began to shrink. This was due in large part to the limited amount of time these busy technology professionals could devote to reading complex information.

Today, the ideal range for a white paper that is targeted to a business professional audience ranges from a bare minimum of four pages to a maximum of twelve pages. As a result, given the limited number of pages associated with these new white papers, marketers realize that they must do more with less than their lengthier predecessors. Since there are fewer pages, each paper must deliver critical business messages quickly and more efficiently to engage the time-challenged, short attention reader.

An Online Design Point

For most of the twentieth century, hard copy printing was part of the traditional white paper development process. During this period, it was assumed that the traditional white paper would be produced by hand (typewriter) and hundreds of copies would be printed (off-set) and distributed by mail (postal service) or via either one-to-one or one-to-many live meetings (seminars, tradeshows, meetings, or sales calls).

With the advent of the Internet in the 1990s, the manual, hard copy methods associated with the traditional white paper gradually began to recede and were replaced with electronic document files that were e-mailed directly to prospective clients or posted on Web sites for a quick download.

Today, the most popular white paper file format is Adobe Acrobat's popular PDF. This format has become popular because a white paper writer using either a Windows PC, Macintosh, or Linux-based computer can create and save a document as a PDF and have that document read by a user with a completely different computer platform different from the one that was originally used to create it. For example, I can create a white paper using a Macintosh, and someone reading my white paper can open it using a Windows PC, Macintosh, Linux computer, or even a handheld device such as an iPhone or Blackberry.

The beauty of a PDF file is that all of the fonts, graphics, text formatting, illustrations, margin settings, etc. are retained with that document. This solved a big problem encountered by early computer users in the 1980s and 1990s. In those days, all computers had to have the same fonts installed as the ones used by the original document creator. If they didn't, the document would substitute different font types, dramatically changing the look and feel of the document.

The vast majority of online document resources such as white paper syndicators, online libraries, Web sites, blogs, online forums, and social media resources have made PDFs a universal standard so users no longer have to worry about the configuration of their computers to retain the original integrity of a white paper. This common file format has made the idea of printing out hard copy versions of a white paper virtually obsolete. It has also dramatically increased the audience for each white paper. Therefore, using PDF, the design point of a White Paper 2.0 document has become the Internet rather than the printing press, and marketers must now ensure that their white papers are enhanced for an audience that predominantly likes to read information online.

While there is still a small and shrinking segment of business readers that like to print documents and read them offline, it continues to be an even smaller segment of the general business audience. Instances for hard copy printing includes support for tradeshows, live seminars, or one-on-one sales calls and meetings. Beyond this segment, the only aspect that most white paper marketers will still need to consider when they develop a white paper is how the document will look when it is printed on a local ink or laser printer that is connected to the reader's computing device.

A Greater Use of Color

Black text on a white background used to be the norm for the traditional white paper throughout most of the twentieth century. In fact many traditional white paper marketers grew accustomed to the typewriter-style fonts of their predecessors and mimicked that look with the advent of the personal computer in the 1980s. Even today, fonts such as Courier or Times Roman remain popular with traditional audiences in the government, academic, and scientific sectors.

Beyond the issue of black serif fonts, these traditional white papers also lacked the use of color in any form, such as graphics, diagrams, and photographs (if and when the technology was available to allow them to have it).

With technology now accelerating the look and feel of the white paper medium, any marketer can now easily accommodate colorful business information. This not only includes formal business information such as charts, graphs, and colored text but also includes stock photography and illustrations to build greater affinity with business readers. For example, if a white paper is targeted to older C-Level business executives, such as a CEOs, COOs, CFOs, etc., the use of professional imagery not only engages readers but also makes them feel more comfortable with the white paper. With greater reader affinity, the deliver of key business messages becomes easier and more effective.

If the goal of a White Paper 2.0 strategy is to attract the short attention reader, colorful information must now be considered an integral component and not an afterthought. Just as we are attracted to colorful, interactive Web sites, as opposed to simple text site maps, short attention readers will seek colorful information as one measure of whether it is worth the investment of their time to read a greater portion of that white paper. Without it, most short attention readers will simply pass on either downloading and/or reading a significant portion of a black and white, all-text white paper. Therefore color must now be considered a required element in a White Paper 2.0 strategy.

The Application of Layout and Design

In the early part of the twentieth century, color was not only expensive to produce, but it was associated with advertisements and art. As a result, the use of layout, design, illustrations, and graphic images was considered marketing fluff, discrediting the viability of "serious" business information. In the minds of the twentieth century business reader, the only way that fact-based information could be delivered to a serious reading audience was to apply pure black text on a white background or else risk Their professional image with that reader.

The advent of the Internet blew this theory out of the water. The use of layout, design, illustrations, and graphic images with today's colorful Web pages has made the acceptance of graphically formatted information not only a reality but also an accepted and expected way to deliver information to a Web-savvy business reader. Therefore, a White Paper 2.0 strategy is akin to that line from the popular 1960s movie *Mary Poppins*, "A spoonful of sugar helps the medicine go down." By incorporating professional layout and design to a white paper, the complex, technical, and/or detailed information contained in a white paper becomes more attractive and compelling to the short attention reader. This makes it easier for the information to be read, assimilated, and clearly understood.

Take a look at the two white papers on the next page that were recently downloaded from the popular social media Web site, Twitter. Which one do you think today's business reader would be more willing to download and read in-depth?

The answer of course is the one on the right-hand side. The use of professional imagery, layout, and design in a White Paper 2.0 strategy will generate greater reader attention, increasing the willingness of readers to open the document and become more engaged with its content. This has now become the new norm with the short attention reader. Without it, the chances of building a similar level of engagement and affinity decrease using a traditional all-text format.

Traditional Text vs. a Graphic White Paper 2.0 Format

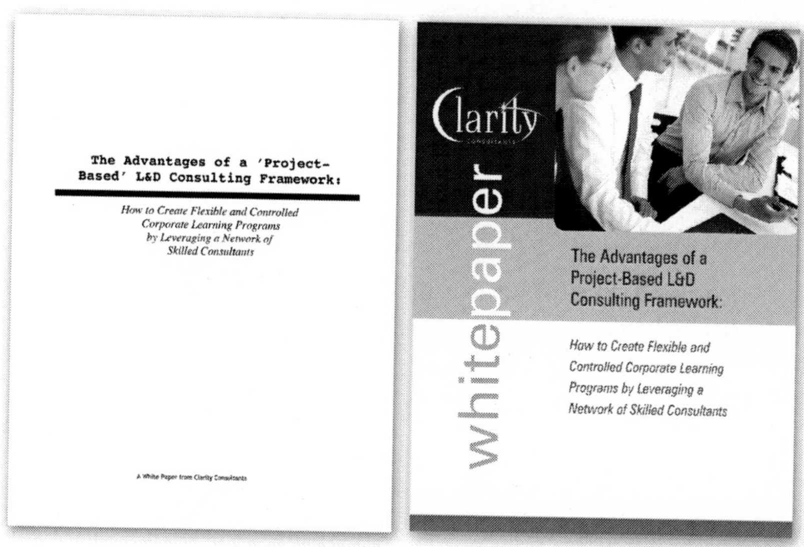

Graphic design makes delivering solution messages much easier.

Attention-Oriented Text Enhancements

As the traditional white paper evolved from its origins as a mono-font document into one that uses several fonts, sizes, and colors, the ability to grab the attention of the reader has correspondingly improved. This evolution has also incorporated other text-oriented enhancements over the years since to further improve reader attention and the delivery of essential business messages.

A text enhancement is characterized as a white paper technique that makes a text- oriented business or solution message easier to read for a short attention reader. For example, if we were describing how to bake an apple pie, one approach might be to describe each ingredient using one long contiguous paragraph, with each ingredient on a single line, using commas to separate them. As an alternative, a text-enhanced approach would be to list each ingredient separately using a table or bullet format so the recipe can be easier to read and use. Instead of using bold or underlining in the hope that the reader will notice and read that text, a text-enhanced approach would be to enlarge and insert that sentence in either the left or right margin so it stands out and is more easily noticed by the reader. There are several of these text-enhanced approaches that can be applied within a White Paper 2.0 strategy, which ensures that critical solution-oriented messages will be more easily noticed, read, and understood by a short attention reader.

Online Sharing and Distribution

During the period of the traditional white paper, the concept of distribution applied to the number of white papers that could be physically printed, mailed, and handed out to a willing audience within the writer's local proximity. Now with the Internet, white papers can be e-mailed, posted to a Web site, blog, or online forum, and downloaded to thousands or millions of readers across the globe. The design of a white paper to better accommodate these online resources has now become an essential part of an effective White Paper 2.0 strategy.

Chapter 9: Forming Your White Paper 2.0 Subject Strategy

An effective White Paper 2.0 strategy is designed to address current issues that are on the minds of a current or prospective business audience. Two of the most frequently asked questions for any business marketer that has decided to add white papers to their marketing plan is what do I write about, and what should I write first?

To answer these important questions and determine the subject(s) for your White Paper 2.0 strategy, businesses typically will use one of two different approaches: a top-down subject strategy or a bottom-up subject strategy. Here is an explanation of each one and how they play an important role in a White Paper 2.0 business plan:

A "Top-Down" White Paper Strategy is determined by the executive management team of an organization and is designed to support critical and timely enterprise business issues that management deems important. For example, if the marketing team is planning on a new product rollout or campaign in the future, a white paper can be timed to coincide with the timeline of that rollout. On a more tactical level, events such as tradeshows, seminars, closing a large prospective customer, or rolling out a new version of a product or service could also warrant the development of a white paper. On another level, a white paper could be developed to educate and inform an existing customer base of a merger or acquisition. In either case, the topic(s) selected comes from the top of the organization and filter down to lower management and employee levels for implementation.

A "Bottom-Up" White Paper Strategy for white paper topics is determined by the employees of an organization that are in the best position to identify and determine customer requirements and needs. Using this approach, the white paper topics are based on current market issues or competitive threats that the customer deems important. For example, if the sales force is hearing from their customers that social media is important and they are inquiring what the organization's plans are for social media integration, that topic might be a good candidate for a white paper. A bottom-up white paper strategy requires a well-managed communication and feedback loop between all departments that interface with the customer, including customer support, sales, technical support, and marketing. To ensure the effectiveness of a bottom-up strategy, the management team must listen to customer issues and be willing to implement a white paper strategy to address them.

Chapter 10: White Paper 2.0—Six Elements for Reader Attention

Today we live in a sound-bite world that is centered on the concept of abbreviated information. Some examples of abbreviated information that have become part of our daily lives include:

- Headline news updates
- SMS text messages
- Twitter Tweets
- Video sound bites
- Audio podcasts

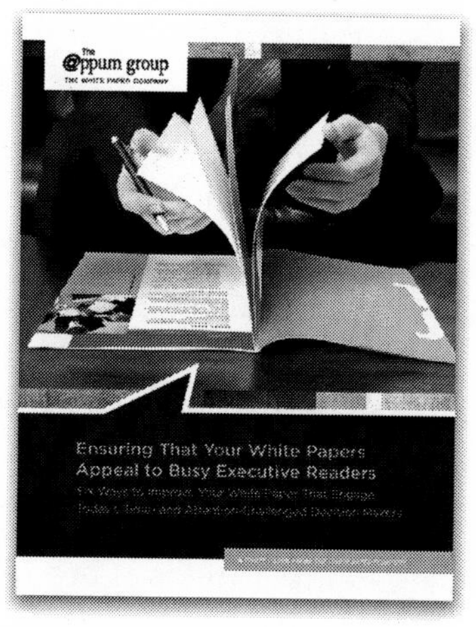

These abbreviated forms of information have become extremely popular due to the limited amount of time that we have made available to read them. The short nature of these abbreviated information sources also allows us to choose the most appropriate time and place for that reading. We don't have to respond to these messages immediately, and we can choose to read them later when we have more time. If we find a particular message interesting, we can read more detailed information by following hyperlinked information associated with that message that leads us to the Web.

For example, we can setup Google Alerts to inform us of the articles that have been posted that meet certain keyword criteria. If we desire more information on that topic, we merely click on a hyperlink associated with that abbreviated message and read the Web-based information connected to that alert. The same relationship can be found on the social media Web site Twitter. Using a variety of viewing tools, such as TweetDeck, we can filter Twitter messages known as "Tweets" that contain a specific keyword, sort those messages, and click on a hyperlink embedded in the ones that we find appealing. These links lead us to a PDF file or Web site attached to that Tweet message, providing us with further information.

This process of enticing readers with short messages and leading them to greater amounts of information is a key principle behind a White Paper 2.0 strategy. Getting readers to the point where they will desire to read a white paper in its entirety is one of the primary challenges that today's white paper marketers face given the limited amount of time and attention that busy executives can devote to the reading process. Today's readers must be engaged before they will decide to invest their valuable time to reading more detailed information. Once that has been achieved, then the reader will devote as much time as will be necessary to complete the entire document. Of course, how to get to that point is, as they say, the "64,000 question." This is where a leader-led, short messaging strategy comes into play.

Today there are six essential white paper elements that you can add to your papers that will engage the attention of executive readers and attract them to your detailed white paper solution messages. Taken together, the application of these six elements, which constitute the basis for a White Paper 2.0 strategy, allows a marketer to engage reader interest, where the delivery of critical business information messages can be facilitated for today's business reader.

These six elements include the following:

- **Executive summaries** give a synopsis of an entire white paper within one concise page.
- **Concluding summaries** include valuable "take away" messages once a white paper has been completed.
- **Callouts/Pull quotes** highlight the single most important point on any specific page.
- **Graphics** show a way to understand complex issues via visual illustrations, charts, and graphics
- **Bullet lists** enable a reader to quickly understand all of the key elements that comprise a complex issue.
- **Shaded text boxes** provide the reader with "bottom-line" summary statements.

The implementation of these elements within a white paper facilitates the marketers' ability to deliver complex and essential solution messages for time- and attention-challenged business readers in three important ways:

- **Increasing reader attention—**Including the six attention-generating elements is an excellent way to grab reader attention and deliver essential solution messages for modern executives.
- **Providing concise messaging—**Only a limited amount of information can be presented within any of the six delivery techniques, following the successful "short and succinct" formula of popular social media and other online communications.
- **Ensuring rapid message assimilation—**By using these six attention-generating elements, you can deliver brief solution messages, ensuring that critical information can be rapidly delivered and assimilated by today's busy executive reader.

Chapter 11: Executive Summaries to Grab Reader Attention

The executive summary represents the most concise and effective way to gain reader attention for your most important white paper business messages and should be considered an integral part of any White Paper 2.0 strategy. In fact, a recent report from *InformationWeek*, entitled "How to Maximize the Use of White Papers in Your B2B Marketing and Sales Process," identified how professional IT buyers were utilizing white papers. According to their findings, approximately 80 percent of the survey respondents indicated that the single most important element that white papers should have is an abstract.[8] To be clear, Merriam-Webster defines the noun *abstract* as "a summary of points (as of a writing), usually presented in skeletal form; also something that summarizes or concentrates the essentials of a larger thing or several things."

From a white paper perspective, most readers don't use the term *abstract*. Instead the word *summary* best represents this concept, also known as the executive summary. Beyond the research, there are three primary reasons why an executive summary should be considered a critical element used to grab and hold reader attention in a white paper:

1. Time Investment—In today's highly competitive business environment, time holds a greater value than money. Therefore, the goal of any business is to provide superior customer service, and in this spirit, white paper marketers should treat the issue of reading time with great respect. The addition of an executive summary supports busy executive readers by providing them with direct answers to their most important business questions while making maximum use of their valuable and limited time. If the executive summary can provide high-quality answers to those questions, then readers will invest a greater portion of that limited time to reading most if not all of a white paper.

2. Positive First Impressions—The executive summary is typically the first page that the reader encounters when opening a white paper. As a result, it is often read in its entirety, something that cannot be said for more detailed white paper pages. As with many business experiences, first impressions are often the most important. By laying out the most important solution points in the executive summary, the reader can obtain a good idea of the quality of information and if the remaining pages of the white paper will follow suit. If the first impression with the executive summary is positive, chances are good that the reader will feel the same way about the rest of the white paper, leading to greater reader engagement and participation.

3. Creating a Subsequent Reading Incentive—Some marketers say that the addition of an executive summary distracts readers and dissuades them from reading the rest of the white paper. This perspective holds the notion that by giving away the most important facts up front in the executive summary, there is no longer an incentive for readers to read the rest of the detailed information in the white paper. In fact, just the opposite is true. If the executive summary is succinct and to the point and it answers basic questions that peaks readers' interest, it will create a desire to read more detailed information. If readers are genuinely interested in finding solutions to solve their business problems, executive summaries create the desire to read more and become more informed.

4. Making No Assumptions—A well-crafted executive summary will not assume that readers know anything about the business environment, problem, or advocated solution. Based on this base-level perspective, a well-written executive summary walks readers through a logical but condensed presentation of information so they can determine if the white paper is worth the investment of their valuable time and attention. Many writers mistakenly assume that readers already know what they know, and as a result they use complex or industry-specific terms without adequate explanation. This alienates readers from the start of the white paper. Such assumptions can result in greater reader confusion.

Executive Summary Analogy: The Appetizer for Your White Paper

In many ways executive summaries are similar to appetizers. For well-traveled restaurant connoisseurs, the appetizer is an early indication of the quality of the subsequent entrée and dessert. If that appetizer is fresh, hot, contains quality ingredients, has visual appeal, and is especially tasty, then the chances are good that the subsequent entrée will probably be of the same quality. On the other hand, if that appetizer tastes like it came out of a can or was kept in a freezer for a week, then it is reasonable to assume that the subsequent entrée and dessert will also be equally poor.

This restaurant analogy is similar to an executive summary in that it creates an incentive, not a disincentive, to read the rest of the white paper. Just as a well-prepared appetizer creates a positive impression and anticipation for the entrée, a well-written executive summary that provides high-quality, essential information and answers primary questions about solution effectiveness will create a desire for the reader to read the rest of the white paper to obtain answers that will solve core business needs.

On the other hand, if your white paper does not contain an executive summary, then readers are forced to read a certain number of detailed white paper pages to uncover bottom line answers to their most important questions. In fact, without an executive summary, readers may not get past the first two or three pages if it is too difficult uncovering those answers. This increases readers' frustration, or worse, the likelihood that they may become distracted by other responsibilities such as returning phone calls, responding to incoming e-mail messages, or attending office meetings.

Any situation where there is a long period of time before readers are engaged with written content will increase the likelihood that they may not be engaged at all. This can lead to one of two outcomes: the decision maker may either forward the white paper to another subordinate within the department/organization or that person may forgo reading the white paper altogether! In either case, the opportunity to influence a strategic decision maker and advance them to a call-to-action response is lost.

Understanding the Two Types of Executive Summaries

There are two types of executive summaries used in white papers, both of which are equally effective in delivering brief but valuable information. These styles are referred to as the Preview-style and the Synopsis-style executive summaries.

Preview-Style Executive Summaries

The Preview-style executive summary is similar to the concept of a movie trailer. Using this style, readers obtain an overview of the white paper content via short, bottom-line, problem-oriented messages that are limited to one complete page. This gives executive readers just enough information to pique their curiosity and create an incentive for them to read the rest of the white paper.

In a movie trailer, viewers are presented with a preview of the crisis and the villain as it relates to the primary theme of the movie. The viewers are not provided with how the crisis is solved or how the movie ends. Within the trailer viewers see a series of carefully chosen segments from the movie, and based on how they are presented, they can determine if there is a desire for them to see the entire film.

The Preview approach as applied to white papers uses one complete page made up of a series of short paragraphs and bulleted statements taken from the white paper that are dedicated to problem assessments and their repercussions.

The Preview-style executive summary starts off with one or two paragraphs that educates on the general market issues, which are followed by a summary of the most important problems associated with the topic related to the previously mentioned market conditions. This is followed by the repercussions or impacts related to those problems.

For example, if we were writing a white paper on the issue of wireless network security, our Preview-style executive summary would discuss:

- **Market Conditions**—What is the current market condition? What factors are taking place within the business environment that causes the problem to occur? (Example: *The rise in online crime in the U.S. and overseas.*)
- **Problem Assessment**—What is at the heart of the situation? What are the specific problems customers experience that need to be resolved and are preventing them from being productive? (Examples: *Security threats such as Trojan Horses, phishing schemes, stealing personal information on corporate databases, malevolent browser cookies*)
- **Causes and Repercussions—**What will happen if nothing is done? What are specific examples that readers should be aware of if they do nothing? (Examples: *Identity theft, lost*

business opportunities, loss of customers, information acquired by competitors)

If executed correctly, the Preview-style executive summary should acknowledge the same problems and/or challenges that readers are facing within their own business environment. This is known as the "head-nod" moment, when readers are able to recognize some of the same problems within their business or industry. This connection builds reader affinity, creating a desire to read additional information in an attempt to uncover solutions to those problem(s). Solutions are not mentioned in the Preview style, only the problem assessments and their repercussions alone. Therefore, it is understood that solutions to the problems can only be achieved by reading the subsequent pages of the white paper content.

The Preview-Style Executive Summary

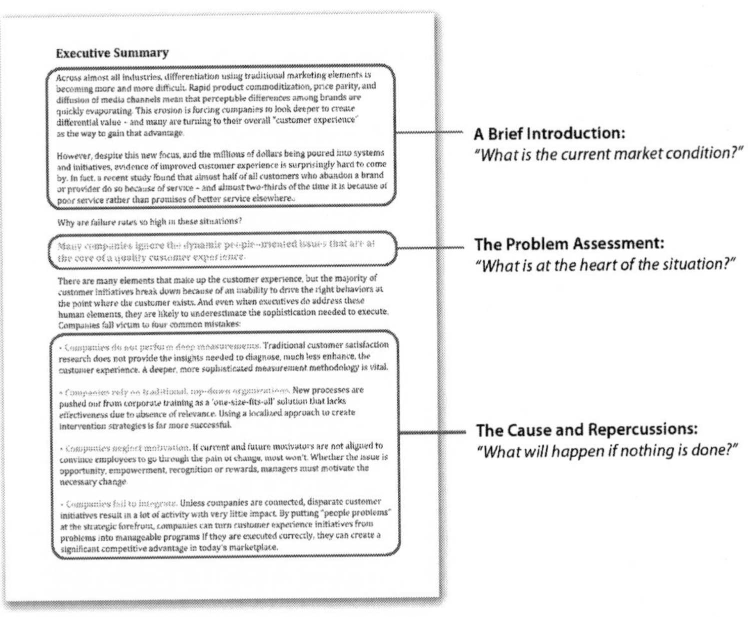

Executive Summary

Across almost all industries, differentiation using traditional marketing elements is becoming more and more difficult. Rapid product commoditization, price parity, and diffusion of media channels mean that perceptible differences among brands are quickly evaporating. This erosion is forcing companies to look deeper to create differential value - and many are turning to their overall "customer experience" as the way to gain that advantage.

However, despite this new focus, and the millions of dollars being poured into systems and initiatives, evidence of improved customer experience is surprisingly hard to come by. In fact, a recent study found that almost half of all customers who abandon a brand or provider do so because of service - and almost two-thirds of the time it is because of poor service rather than promises of better service elsewhere.

Why are failure rates so high in these situations?

Many companies ignore the dynamic people-oriented issues that are at the core of a quality customer experience.

There are many elements that make up the customer experience, but the majority of customer initiatives break down because of an inability to drive the right behaviors at the point where the customer exists. And even when executives do address these human elements, they are likely to underestimate the sophistication needed to execute. Companies fall victim to four common mistakes:

- Companies do not perform deep measurements. Traditional customer satisfaction research does not provide the insights needed to diagnose, much less enhance, the customer experience. A deeper, more sophisticated measurement methodology is vital.

- Companies rely on traditional, top-down organizations. New processes are pushed out from corporate training as a 'one-size-fits-all' solution that lacks effectiveness due to absence of relevance. Using a localized approach to create intervention strategies is far more successful.

- Companies neglect motivation. If current and future motivators are not aligned to convince employees to go through the pain of change, most won't. Whether the issue is opportunity, empowerment, recognition or rewards, managers must motivate the necessary change.

- Companies fail to integrate. Unless companies are connected, disparate customer initiatives result in a lot of activity with very little impact. By putting "people problems" at the strategic forefront, companies can turn customer experience initiatives from problems into manageable programs If they are executed correctly, they can create a significant competitive advantage in today's marketplace.

A Brief Introduction:
"What is the current market condition?"
The Problem Assessment:
"What is at the heart of the situation?"
The Cause and Repercussions:
"What will happen if nothing is done?"

The Preview style uses problem statements to increase content curiosity.

Synopsis-Style Executive Summaries

The Synopsis-style executive summary is a second style that uses a different approach from the Preview-style summary by providing a complete synopsis of the entire white paper in one complete page. The difference with the synopsis approach is that both problems and solutions are presented using four sections that represent the most salient points covered in the white paper. These sections are identified as follows:

1. The Situation (*What is causing the problem*?)—The first segment of the Synopsis-style executive summary focuses on the market/industry issues and/or dynamics that are behind the white paper topic. Situational information can include economic factors, customer demands, or competitive forces that are responsible for the central business issue. For example, if we were writing a white paper on the benefits of a wireless network security solution, our situation might be the rise in identity theft, online credit card crime, network intrusion, or phishing schemes.

2. The Problem (*What is the specific problem*?)—The second portion of the Synopsis-style executive summary highlights the primary business challenge(s) that are related to the situational issue. The problem can be related to one of two situations: the absence of any solution in the marketplace that could solve the situational issue(s) or the inadequacy of existing solutions to address those issues. Using our wireless network security analogy, a problem statement for this section of the executive summary might be that existing wireless network security solutions cannot be upgraded in a timely manner to adequately address the pace in which new security threats are appearing on the Internet.

3. The Solution (*How is the problem resolved*?)—This portion of the Synopsis-style executive summary states the recommended solution designed to solve the previously described business challenges and/or problems. The solution statement can be in one of two different forms: it can identify the solution by name or apply a high-level, generic approach. Given the one-page limitation, the description of the solution needs to be short and succinct. This approach depends on the marketing strategy of the white paper marketer. Some organizations prefer to identify the solution by name. Others, fearing that disclosing a solution name is akin to an overt sales pitch, prefer the use of generic descriptions. If a reader is genuinely interested in solving an existing business problem, mentioning a solution name should not dissuade the reader from reading the entire white paper.

Using the previous analogy of wireless network security, the solution advantage section would describe how the network security solution solved the previously identified problem.

4. The Result (*What is the benefit from the solution*?)—This portion of the Synopsis-style executive summary would describe the specific results that would be gained from the implementation of the recommended solution. The results can be described several ways: the gains made financially (profits), the (re)allocation of resources (utilization/lower costs), time reductions (shortened windows of opportunity or time to market), or labor savings (fewer or more efficient employees). Again, with the network security analogy, this section would describe the benefits realized after implementation of the solution. The following is an illustration of a Synopsis-style executive summary page:

The Synopsis-Style Executive Summary

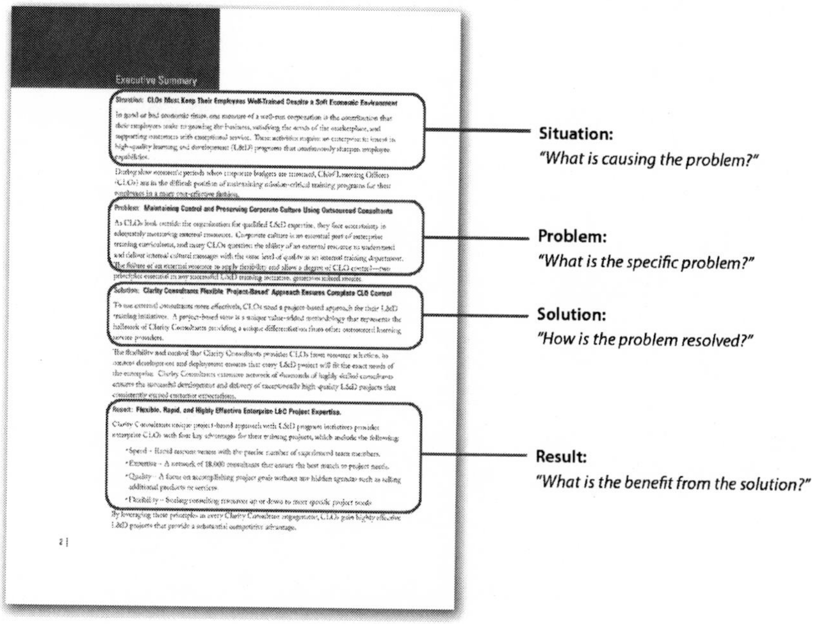

Situation:
"What is causing the problem?"

Problem:
"What is the specific problem?"

Solution:
"How is the problem resolved?"

Result:
"What is the benefit from the solution?"

Synopsis style summarizes a white paper into four distinct sections.

Executive Summary Formatting Techniques

With a one-page restriction, it is important to format summary information in a way that will quickly grab reader attention and allow readers to maximize their interest in not only reading the entire executive summary but also in reading the subsequent sections of the white paper. Each of the two executive summaries has formatting techniques that will help white paper marketers achieve this goal.

- **Limit to One Page**—Keep the information to one page to maintain reader attention without overwhelming them with too much information.
- **Clearly Identify Key Points**—Make sure each of the key points identified in the executive summary clearly

represents existing issues that the reader is facing while presenting short, succinct, and logical answers that will solve them.

- **Use Headlines**—Use one-line statements that summarize each situation, problem, solution, and result point.
- **Create Distinct Sections**—Create separate sections for background issues, problem assessments, solution advantages, and summary points by using spacing between each section. This ensures that your readers will be able to separate each message or jump to the ones that are most important to their company/marketplace.
- **Large Fonts/Colors**—Choose larger fonts or different colors to identify portions such as header names, headlines, or bottom-line information so that critical messages can be easily seen.

A Summary on Executive Summaries

The use of an executive summary quickly grabs reader attention, thereby allowing time- and attention-challenged executive readers to determine whether the white paper will be a good investment of their limited and valuable time. More importantly, the information contained in an executive summary allows readers to quickly determine if the white paper will solve their existing business needs.

The executive summary does not dissuade reader interest in the primary sections of the white paper. Instead, a logically produced and well-written executive summary creates an incentive for the reader to greater portions of the white paper content. If the issues presented in the summary make sense to readers and accurately identify their current situation and/or problems, readers that are genuinely interested in solving an existing business problem *will* seek additional information to solve it. As a result, readers that can obtain answers to their most important questions in the executive summary will be naturally inclined to read the rest of the white paper to obtain detailed answers that will solve those problems.

The effectiveness with the executive summary's ability to grab reader attention and create an incentive to read more detailed sections of a white paper fulfills the primary goal of a White Paper 2.0 strategy. White paper marketers seeking to make their white papers more effective with a short attention reading audience should seriously consider adding this technique to their white paper arsenal.

Chapter 12: Concluding Summaries—Not Last, But Often First

What's the difference between the executive summary and the concluding summary? This is a question frequently asked by many white paper readers and marketers.

First, the executive summary assumes that readers know nothing about the white paper topic and provides them with introductory and background information that create an incentive to read the rest of the document. In comparison, the concluding summary assumes readers have read the entire white paper, and as a result, reinforces essential "take away" messages that readers should have retained when finished.

While most people would assume that the concluding summary would be one of the last sections read in the white paper, it is often one of the first areas noticed by the skim reader, someone who quickly flips through a white paper upon initial exposure to the document.

As the skim reader is glancing through the various pages of the white paper, the concluding summary page provides a natural stopping point, since it is the last page of the document. As a result, readers tend to spend more time on this page. This natural stop provides white paper marketers with an important opportunity to deliver essential solution advantage messages. A well-written concluding summary also increases the chance that skim readers will advance to the second, preliminary reading stage where they can determine the validity of the white paper to meet their critical business needs. This marketing opportunity makes the concluding summary an important part of a White Paper 2.0 strategy.

A well-executed concluding summary contains three important basic elements that capture reader attention during this natural stopping point: key take away messages, elevator pitch statements, and call-to-action information.

Key Take Away Messages

A take away message is something the white paper reader should retain after reading the primary content of the white paper. Take away messages don't have to be focused solely on solution advantages. They can also represent problem assessments that the white paper solution is designed to solve. For many readers, problem issues often resonate more strongly than solution advantage messages, creating an incentive for the reader to become more closely engaged with the primary white paper content.

Within the concluding summary, several ideas for take away messages might include:

- The most important market issue causing the current problem or situation
- The biggest reason why competing solutions aren't adequately addressing this situation
- Why the solution strategy is best qualified to meet and address the situational problem

In each instance, these take away points should reinforce and reiterate the same messages that have been delivered in the primary sections of the white paper. The concept is akin to the idea of leveraged learning, or building on what the reader already has learned. But there is an important point to remember: you do not want to bring up an entirely new message in this section that has not been previously addressed in the main white paper sections. To do so will only confuse your readers and blur the most important points that you want them to retain after they finish the paper.

To give your take away messages greater impact, it is recommended that you use the same copy from the main sections of your white paper but change the copy slightly so those same points will not seem repetitious to your readers.

Elevator Pitch Statements

What is an elevator pitch statement? The term comes from a classic sales technique of the same name. Imagine that you are a salesman riding an elevator with an executive decision maker from a company that you would like to have as a customer. What would you tell that executive between floors 1 and 20 that would cause him or her to grant you an appointment to discuss your solution? Those quickly delivered and carefully chosen words constitute your elevator pitch.

Elevator pitch statements are typically presented in bullet lists or short bulleted paragraphs. Bullets are an important formatting element for the short attention reader because the dots or symbols at the front of the statement attract attention on an otherwise stark page of paragraph-oriented text. (How to use bullets effectively will be discussed in detail in a subsequent chapter of this book.)

Since elevator pitches are frequently found on the concluding summary page, it becomes a critical location to remind readers of the most important points they have already read. This is also an important landing spot for skim readers who may have missed those points after reviewing them during their first exposure to the document.

Elevator pitch statements are typically three or four summary points followed by one brief sentence that explains each issue in greater detail. Elevator pitch statements also translate solution elements into business advantages that are typically expressed as a function of people, money, time, resources, profitability, ROI, etc. Here is an example of a simple three-part elevator pitch you would find in a concluding summary:

To summarize, Acme Widgets provides enterprise businesses with three key advantages:

- *Greater Productivity*—Acme Widgets design fosters greater ease of use, which translates into greater worker productivity.
- *Faster Market Responsiveness*—Acme Widgets creates more efficient workflows between groups, which shortens the time to deployment and allows for faster market responsiveness.
- *Faster Return on Investment (ROI)*—The cost savings associated with the implementation of Acme Widgets generates a faster return on investment, which contributes to greater profitability.

Call-to-Action Information

Call-to-action information is another important element of a strong White Paper 2.0 strategy. The call-to-action section of the concluding summary is where you "ask for the order" and hopefully create an incentive for the reader to initiate action such as contacting the sponsor or visiting a Web site. The important information that should be included in the call-to-action section includes the following:

- **About the author statement/paragraph**—This can be information from your Web site, where you discuss the history, philosophy, or other information about the solution provider represented in the white paper.
- **Contact directions**—This is a statement of direction that includes the Web site URL, phone number, e-mail address, or fax number. The statement usually starts with "For more information about Acme Widgets, please contact us at ____________________."

- **A contact block**—A block of information at the bottom of the page that includes your corporate street address, department name, P.O. box, city, state, and zip code. You can also repeat your Web site URL and/or phone number in this block.

Your concluding summary is more than a simple closing statement to your white paper. By including a variety of attention-generating information, you can leverage your concluding summary into a section that not only grabs reader attention early in the skim reading process but also provides a way for your reader to remember your primary solution advantage points after the paper has been completely read.

Chapter 13: Callouts—The First Item Noticed on the Page

Callouts (also known as pull quotes) serve as an essential part of any White Paper 2.0 strategy. The term refers to the portions of text that are found in the sidebar margins of a white paper page that showcase the most important point that has been made on that page. Callouts are one distinct element that clearly differentiates second-generation (2.0) white papers from traditional all-text white papers.

The Sidebar Callout

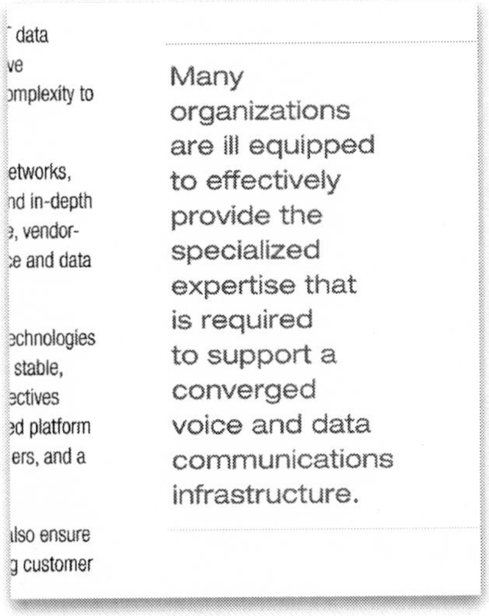

Many organizations are ill equipped to effectively provide the specialized expertise that is required to support a converged voice and data communications infrastructure.

Callouts isolate key business messages so they can be easily understood.

With a callout, portions of text are being "called out," or isolated, from the primary white paper content that is on the page. Within a commercial white paper, callouts can be statements, statistics, or actual quotes from a leading authority on the topic.

The reason that callouts are essential is that they are often one of the first things noticed on a white paper page. Callouts are quickly noticed because the text sits alone within an open white space on the sidebar margin. Since callouts often use larger font sizes than the primary content, they have a higher likelihood of being noticed and read.

Here are some tips to keep in mind for the proper use of callouts:

1. Keep It Short—A callout should be as short as possible since the marketer only has few valuable seconds of undivided reader attention. It should contain no more than a sentence, using anywhere from ten to twenty words.

2. Format to Grab Attention—A callout should use formatting that clearly separates it from the font/size/style/color used in the adjacent body copy. While the surrounding white space will ensure that the callout is noticed, applying additional text formatting will ensure that the marketing message contained in the callout will be noticed.

3. Apply Frequently—Callouts should be used on every page if possible, especially if that page contains nothing more than left-flush, paragraph-oriented text. In these situations, the use of a callout or pull quote breaks up the monotony of repetitious formatting, which often contributes to reader boredom and detachment. It also ensures that important business messages will be delivered if nothing else is read on that page.

Some Important Notes

For sections that contain bullet lists, graphic elements, charts, tables, or other attention-generating items, it is advisable not to place a callout on that page since there will be other reader distractions.

In addition, it is not advisable to have more than one callout on a page, since they will also create greater reader distractions. This approach robs the graphic or table from its share of reader attention. It's always best to apply a "less is more" strategy—use callouts on pages where they can stand out on a page of standard text paragraphs.

Finally, with so much attention devoted to the callout, the portion of text that you dedicate to this task should be the single most important message on that page. Candidate text for a callout includes:

- A sentence that best summarizes the assessment of the main business challenge/problem
- A sentence that best summarizes the solution to a previously mentioned problem
- A quote used in the white paper that comes from a credible or recognized source

The callout/pull quote you select should depend on your topic and your message delivery goals.

The Callout/Pull Quote Editor

When you place a callout in its own white space within the sidebar margin, a funny thing happens. It is read more closely than if that sentence was embedded within a paragraph in the middle of the page. In these circumstances, you may find yourself editing the callout, and as a result rewriting the original sentence in order to make both the callout and the paragraph more effective.

Not only does the callout result in subsequent editing of the original sentence, but you may also find yourself using an abbreviated form of the original sentence for your callout. Here's an example of a sentence in a white paper that was chosen for a sidebar callout:

> *"Acme Consulting Group has been the leading provider of project-based training programs for over 16 years, with an extensive network comprising thousands of highly qualified consultants that satisfies the needs of any enterprise training project."*

Clearly, this sentence is too large to accommodate a sidebar callout. While we may not necessarily want to reduce the size of this sentence within the body copy, we can use a portion of this text in our callout and still create the effectiveness needed to draw attention to its central message. With this in mind, our modified callout using only a portion of the previous sentence would now read:

> *Acme Consulting Group has been the leading provider of project-based training programs, with an extensive network comprising thousands of highly qualified consultants.*

This revised sentence is much shorter, easier to read, and succinct. We are able to accomplish two simultaneous tasks with this change: 1) drawing reader attention to the callout on the page, while 2) educating the reader to a key solution message in the primary body copy.

Serial Callout Storytelling

White Paper 2.0 writers need to view the white paper in the same light as their readers and make modifications to the paper that will ensure easier reader comprehension of critical solution messages.

It is common knowledge that most readers skim a white paper when they first open it, and callouts are one of the first items they notice while doing so. It also stands to reason that taken together as one collective group, the white paper callouts should reinforce a unified and cohesive message. This is something that I refer to as "serial callout storytelling."

Serial Sidebar Callouts

Many organizations are ill equipped to effectively provide the specialized expertise that is required to support a converged voice and data communications infrastructure.

Multiple callouts read together provide a succinct business message.

Serial callout storytelling is the ability to read each callout in an entire white paper in the order they have been presented and determine the primary solution message(s) that they represent.

Try this exercise with your next white paper project that uses embedded callouts. Read only the callouts that are found in the paper, starting with the introduction and continuing to each of the subsequent pages. Then ask yourself the following questions based on your first impression of those callouts:

- Did you understand the primary message(s) in the white paper?
- Were they in a logical order and did they make sense?
- Did they consistently reinforce the same theme in the white paper?
- Were you more interested in reading the rest of the white paper as a result of reading the callouts?

If your answer to any of these questions is "No," or "I'm not sure," then you may have selected the wrong callouts for your pages and may want to go back and change them. On the other hand, if you have a general idea of the white paper, then you have made good choices of callouts for your content pages. After all, if you can't understand the primary message conveyed by the callouts, why should your readers, especially if they have no prior knowledge with the topic?

The Header/Callout Connection

After the callout, what's the next most noticeable item on a white paper page? Answer: The Section Header.

With these two items acting as the most noticed elements on the white paper page, there is a natural connection that occurs between them. Therefore, your callout should not only highlight the most important message on the page, but it should also address the proposition made by the section header.

The example below shows a section that is entitled, "The Value of Employee Benefit Benchmarking." Also on that same page, a callout has been chosen that answers the issue posed by the header and defines what the value of the employee program is. Since these two elements are the first items noticed on this page, the ability for the white paper writer to select the best sentence that will closely align the callout to the header increases the odds that the reader will notice them. It also creates an incentive to read the entire section and, quite possibly, the rest of the white paper.

Aligning the Section Header and the Callout/Pull Quote

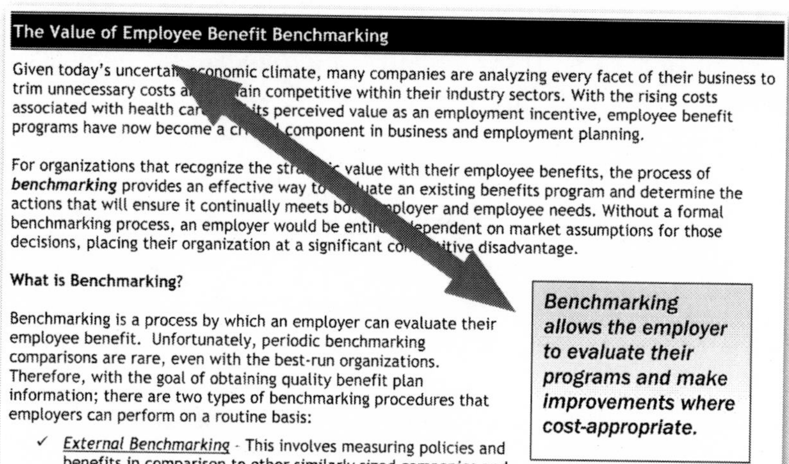

The Value of Employee Benefit Benchmarking

Given today's uncerta[illegible]conomic climate, many companies are analyzing every facet of their business to trim unnecessary costs a[illegible]ain competitive within their industry sectors. With the rising costs associated with health car[illegible]ts perceived value as an employment incentive, employee benefit programs have now become a c[illegible] component in business and employment planning.

For organizations that recognize the str[illegible] value with their employee benefits, the process of ***benchmarking*** provides an effective way t[illegible]uate an existing benefits program and determine the actions that will ensure it continually meets bo[illegible]ployer and employee needs. Without a formal benchmarking process, an employer would be enti[illegible]pendent on market assumptions for those decisions, placing their organization at a significant co[illegible]itive disadvantage.

What is Benchmarking?

Benchmarking is a process by which an employer can evaluate their employee benefit. Unfortunately, periodic benchmarking comparisons are rare, even with the best-run organizations. Therefore, with the goal of obtaining quality benefit plan information; there are two types of benchmarking procedures that employers can perform on a routine basis:

✓ *External Benchmarking* - This involves measuring policies and benefits in comparison to other similarly sized companies and

Benchmarking allows the employer to evaluate their programs and make improvements where cost-appropriate.

Align headers to create greater reader engagement with content.

Netting Out the Callout Issue

As with any visual element, there is a point where its repetitive use can result in a negative impact on the reader. In many ways using too many callouts is akin to "crying wolf," where readers become turned off to their messages. How do you know if you have either the right callouts or too many? Here are some guidelines to follow as you employ this important element to engage readers toward your white paper callout messages:

1. **Don't use more than one callout per page**—Too many callouts will draw attention away from the single most important point on the white paper content page. This is a perfect example of the popular phase "less is more." One single callout on a page that has a unique format (font size, lines, boxes, etc.) will have a much greater impact on reader engagement than two or three on the same page.

2. **Make sure you apply the most important message, not trivial information**—The message that you choose for your callout should represent a key problem or solution point that supports the main white paper topic. This can be a key industry quote, a statistic, a research finding, or a bottom-line point associated with the problem assessment or solution advantage message.
3. **Make it visually stand out**—Since the goal is gaining greater reader attention, apply mechanisms to gain that attention. Suggestions include increasing the font size of the callout at least one size greater than the adjacent body copy (often 12- or 14-point text). Use boxes, lines, shading, or other visual treatments to ensure that those messages will be noticed.
4. **Think of your readers' needs and choose what's most important to them**—Don't choose text that you may think is important or what will fulfill the goals of your marketing plan. Instead, put yourself in the position of your readers and choose your callouts based on what you think will be most important to them in solving their specific business needs.
5. **Keep it short—one sentence with no more than twenty words**—There is a limited amount of time to gain reader attention on any white paper page. If necessary, trim down an important sentence to less than twenty words within that callout if you want your short attention reader to notice it and assimilate your critical solution message.

Chapter 14: Graphics—Visual Reader Engagement

To reiterate our previously used quote, "A picture is worth a thousand words." But how much are a thousand words worth?

In terms of time, it's probably about five seconds. That's the amount of time that a reader will spend reading the first sentence of that 1000-word article to determine if it's worth reading the other 990.

That's why we are drawn to graphic images, design, and illustrations. We notice them from the start, along with the information that they impart. They get our attention, engage us, and as a result, we will look at pictures for a longer period of time than a similar portion of text. If it works for a magazine, a Web site, or a blog, then it stands to reason that will also work for a white paper, especially given our limited amount of time and attention for reading large volumes of detailed text.

While the copy in your white paper may be grammatically correct, writing alone is not enough to yield an effective white paper, since today's reader no longer reads a white paper in its entirety. Today, elements such as document design, the creation of concept/business graphics, and illustrations are the new requirements to get readers attention, draw them into content, and enable them to assimilate critical business messages. Graphics are certainly a critical element in an effective White Paper 2.0 strategy.

If your white paper does not incorporate elements such as design and graphics, you are probably not making the strongest connection with your white paper readers. As a result, you may not be effectively promoting your company, brand, solution, or strategy given the limited amount of time they will spend reading your white paper.

While graphics can vary from one white paper to another, in keeping with the development of a White Paper 2.0 strategy, this book will focus on four content-related graphics that can be added to your white paper to increase reader attention and effectiveness. These four graphic elements not only represent the most frequently used graphics today but also the most effective in appealing to today's short attention span executive reader. These are:

- Concept graphics
- Business charts
- Workflow graphics
- Screenshot graphics

Concept Graphics

When it comes to incorporating graphics into a white paper, marketers have a wide variety of choices. In fact, if you've seen the current list of charting options in your favorite spreadsheet application, it might be slightly intimidating to know exactly how and when to use each one.

If the goal of a white paper is grabbing the attention of a short attention executive reader, the list of the most effective graphic versions becomes much shorter. One that clearly rises to the top of that list is the concept graphic, which is an important component in any well-executed White Paper 2.0 strategy.

What Is a Concept Graphic?

A concept graphic (like the image below) is a business illustration that translates a complex, multifaceted business concept into a simple visual form. The goal with any concept graphic is not only to educate readers but also to grab their attention in the hope that it will compel them to read the accompanying text that is adjacent to it.

Concept graphics can be used to illustrate a corporate philosophy, a business strategy, a current business or marketplace situation, or even an existing business problem or challenge.

An Example of a Concept Graphic

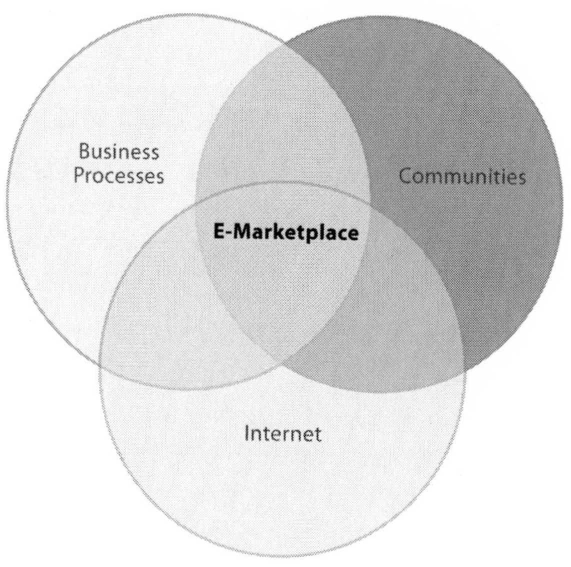

Concept graphics illustrate the components of complex relationships into a simpler visual form.

What Are the Elements of a Good Concept Graphic?

The idea behind a concept graphic is that well-worn business axiom, K.I.S.S., or "Keep it Simple and Straightforward." A concept graphic should educate your white paper reader to the central business message without any accompanying text.

For example, the concept graphic pictured on the previous page tells us that e-marketplaces are the integration of three key elements: the Internet, business processes, and (online) communities. Readers don't have to read any additional text to understand the concept highlighted in the Ballentine graphic. All they have to do is look closely at the elements in the concept graphic to understand how the three components are related to one another.

If short attention readers see a concept graphic during their initial skim reading process, the chances are pretty good that they will stop, take notice of that graphic element, and hopefully read the accompanying text that comes before and after that graphic. If this happens with your white paper reader then you have effectively applied concept graphics within your white paper.

To ensure that your concept graphics are successful, here are three tips that you can apply as part of your White Paper 2.0 strategy:

1. Have a Minimum Number of Components and Colors—An important part of a K.I.S.S. strategy is creating a concept graphic with a minimal number of components. As the concept graphic is being developed, white paper marketers must constantly find new ways to reduce the total number of components. This can include several tactics such as consolidating categories, combining data points, or eliminating non-relevant elements. The simpler the design of the concept graphic, the quicker the reader will notice it. This makes it easier for the reader to assimilate the most important business message(s) associated with it.

The same idea applies to the use of color. A concept graphic should use primary colors that not only look good on a color screen, but also replicate well if your white paper is printed on a black and white printer. Since white papers are often passed along to other decision makers in the same organization, creating your concept graphic for both on-screen and hard copy will maximize its effectiveness.

For example, dark reds, purples, and pinks often wash out on a B&W printer, especially if that image incorporates embedded text. When planning a concept graphic, use light shades of green, blue, or orange, because they will look equally well on the screen as they do in print.

2. Employ a 3:1 Graphic-to-Page Ratio—In just about any situation too much of something is never a sound practice. The same is true for the number of graphics that are used in a white paper, especially concept graphics. If too many concept graphics are used, then there is a risk the white paper will look like a PowerPoint presentation, and the reader will quickly become overwhelmed with too much visual stimuli. When this occurs the opportunity to influence readers with key business messages will be lost.

To ensure that this doesn't happen, writers should apply a 3:1 ratio between the number of graphics and the number of pages in your white paper. For example, in a ten-page white paper, use no more than three graphic elements. If the white paper has only six pages, on the other hand, then two graphic elements would be appropriate.

3. Embed Descriptive Labels to Ensure Reader Comprehension

Unfortunately, if a business graphic sits alone on a white paper page without any supporting descriptions, the chances that the short attention reader will flip to the next page increase dramatically. As a result, white paper marketers will lose a valuable opportunity to deliver a key solution message and/or further engage the reader.

To help white paper marketers overcome these mistakes, use descriptive text boxes within sections of the graphic that focus reader attention to special areas of interest and reinforce the titles and subtitles. The use of text boxes ensures that these primary messages will be clearly understood by the white paper reader. For business charts, use a legend whenever possible to ensure your reader understands the relationship between sets of data, especially when those data sets use mixed graphic elements, such as line graphs and column charts.

Traditional Business Charts vs. Esoteric Business Graphics

The principal behind the application of business graphics is to illustrate the relationships between a series of static data points. While business graphics have been used in business communications for many years, their use in a White Paper 2.0 strategy is different from a more traditional role since the type, design, and complexity employed is to convey a business concept as quickly as possible for the short attention span reader.

When it comes to incorporating graphics into a white paper, writers have a wide variety of choices. Most white papers employ one of two groups of business graphics: traditional and esoteric business charts.

Traditional business charts are made up of column, bar, pie, and line graphs. Traditional graphic types are not only the most frequently used but also are easily recognized by the business reader. Traditional business charts also make the process of conveying the relationship between data sets and trends easier for the short attention reader.

The same K.I.S.S. design principals that make concept graphics work so effectively in a White Paper 2.0 strategy also apply to the use of traditional business graphics. With traditional business graphics, the use of a minimal number of data points ensures that the white paper reader can easily assimilate complex relationships between those data points.

As the number of data points in a traditional graphic increase, the relationship between those data points becomes more confusing to the business reader. As a general rule, traditional business graphics that use ten data points or less are more effective with a short attention reader. More than ten, and the reader must spend more time analyzing that chart or graphic, diminishing the impact and effectiveness of that chart in its ability to quickly convey a critical business message or data relationship in a white paper.

As you can see from the following enclosed column chart, readers can quickly see the relationship between the various data points, the data trend, and the largest data segment. On the other hand, if this column chart included twenty data points and corresponding columns, the relationship between those data points would be much harder for readers to understand and would require a significant amount of additional time before they could grasp the primary business message. This would defeat the goal of quickly grabbing the attention of the short attention reader and rapidly conveying business messages as part of a White Paper 2.0 strategy.

The Traditional Column Chart

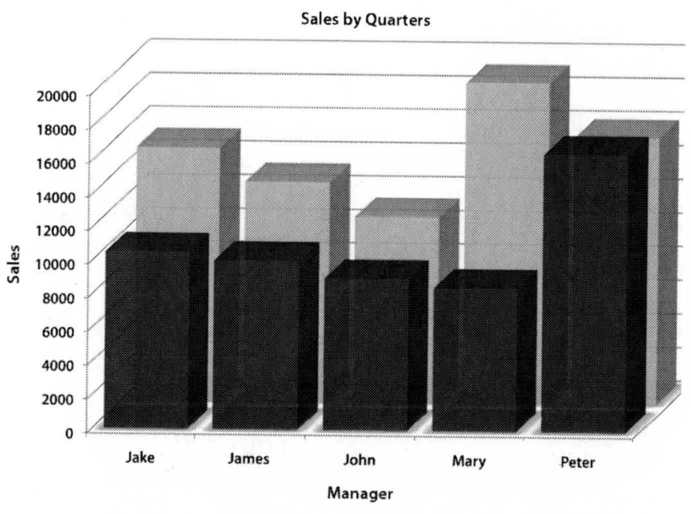

Traditional charts are effective in quickly conveying data relationships.

What Is an Esoteric Business Chart?

Merriam-Webster defines the word *esoteric* as "requiring or exhibiting knowledge that is restricted to a small group." This definition is a perfect fit for this second subset of business graphics that are used in a limited set of business circumstances or with unique data relationships. Types of esoteric business charts include mixed, scatter, radar, bubble, doughnut, and surface.

In most circumstances, esoteric business charts comprise larger sets of data, making the relationship between data points more complex and more confusing for the short attention white paper reader. For example, the radar chart below shows the relationship between ten separate sets of data related to the real estate industry.

With esoteric business charts, it is difficult for the average reader to quickly assimilate important business messages by simply analyzing the graphic alone. When an esoteric business chart is used in a white paper, either a single paragraph or series of paragraphs must accompany that graphic if the reader is going to fully understand the essential business relationships presented in that graphic.

For example, in the radar chart below there are thirteen separate entities that are related to the data, expressed as separate ring segments in the chart. Without any supporting text, it is difficult for a reader to fully understand the relationship between these sets of data and the overall meaning behind the chart. This requires the reader to turn attention away from the graphic and read a significant portion of accompanying text, which may or may not occur. As a result, the use of esoteric business charts must include additional attention-generating elements such as accompanying text, bullets, legends, or callouts to reinforce key solution messages with a short attention reader.

The Esoteric Radar Chart

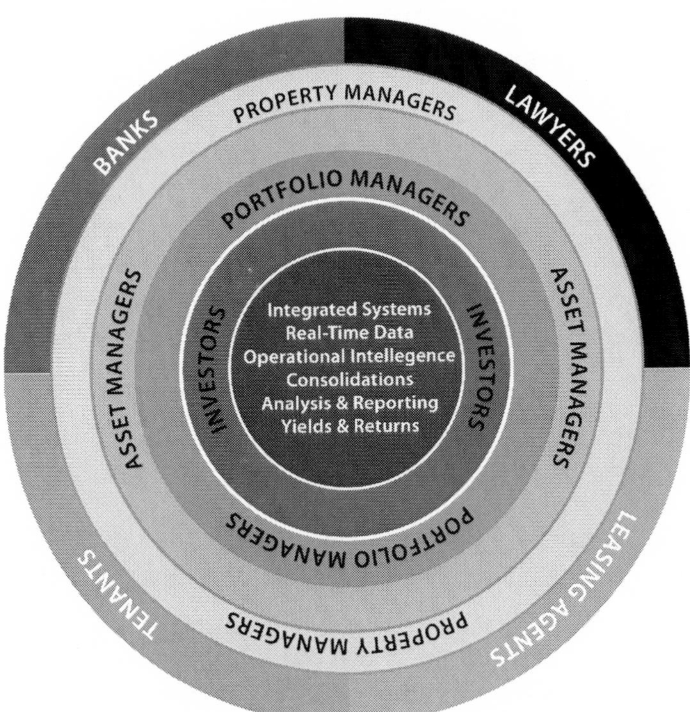

Complex esoteric charts require additional information for the reader.

Workflow Graphics

When there is a need to illustrate the components of a functional process; the details associated with a strategy, business plan, or process; or the orderly progression of tasks that make up a procedure, workflow graphics are a great way to quickly communicate with your short attention reader.

Workflow graphics break down each step that is part of a business process with individual illustrations for each step. Workflow graphics are helpful when applied to manufacturing, software development, or any complex task. For example, the workflow graphic below illustrates the various steps involved in preparing a food management plan.

A Simple Workflow: The Steps in a Food Management Plan

Workflow graphics illustrate multi-element processes and procedures.

Effective workflow graphics designed for the short attention reader should include the following attributes:

- **Simple page width**—All of the components in a workflow graphic should fit across a standard white paper page. If the graphic has several steps and requires an equal number of layers that extend beyond the standard page width, there is higher likelihood that the reader will become disengaged and confused.
- **Clear identification—**Each component in the graphic should be large enough so all elements can be clearly labeled and identified by the reader.
- **Multiple colors/shading—**Using multiple shades or colors allows the reader to easily understand how each element fits into the overall process or procedure.
- **A minimal number of components—**Similar to our strategy with any type of graphic, keeping it simple by applying a minimal number of elements increases the probability that your short attention reader will quickly understand your key solution message(s).

Screenshot Graphics

Screenshot graphics are desktop pictures of an application screen captured using operating system functionality or third-party screen capture utility programs. These programs allow the user to select portions of a software program on the screen and save that captured section as an image file in a variety of popular file formats such as JPEG, GIF, PNG, etc. These files are then trimmed to fit into the width of a white paper page.

Screenshot graphics are helpful to illustrate how that application would perform certain processes that help to educate the white paper reader. But screenshot graphics alone are not enough, and most require several additional elements to provide an adequate level of education for the short attention white paper reader. These additional elements can include the following:

- **Circles**—Highlight the specific element on the screen that you want your readers to notice, otherwise they may not notice what you want them to see.
- **Arrows**—Use an arrow to connect a circle to another element such as a description box.
- **Description Boxes**—Use small portions of text to describe what is in the highlighted screen attribute, what it does, and what its purpose is as described in the primary white paper content.

An example of a screenshot graphic along with an accompanying circle, arrow, and descriptive text box is shown below.

A Screenshot Graphic

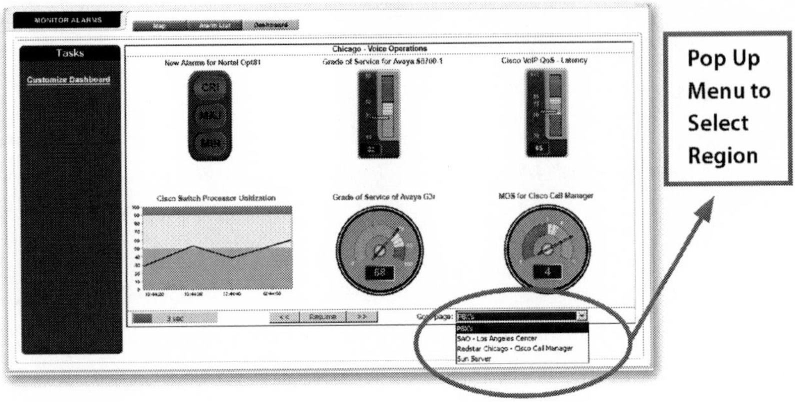

Pop Up Menu to Select Region

Circles and arrows facilitate understanding of screenshot graphics.

How to Effectively Use Descriptions in Your Business Graphics

Visual elements such as business graphics are an excellent way to help a white paper reader understand complex or highly technical issues. This makes it a critical aspect of using graphics effectively in a White Paper 2.0 strategy.

In many white papers, business graphics are placed in the middle of two text paragraphs without the support of descriptions that would otherwise help the reader easily understand the primary message associated with that chart or graphic. Many white paper writers assume that the reader already knows what the graphic represents, and as a result, leave out supporting descriptions for the business chart. Many white paper marketers also assume that the reader will read *all* of the accompanying text placed either before and/or after the chart.

These assumptions do not take into consideration skim readers, who flip through the white paper pages immediately after their first exposure to the document. During this preliminary scanning phase, skim readers are looking for visual elements such as graphics or text that will capture their attention and engage their interest to read an additional amount of detailed information.

Unfortunately, if a business graphic sits alone on a white paper page without any supporting descriptions, the chances that a skim reader will flip to the next page increases dramatically. As a result, white paper marketers will lose a valuable opportunity to utilize that graphic and deliver an essential solution message to further engage the reader.

To help white paper marketers overcome these mistakes, there are several tips that can help create more effective descriptions when business or concept graphics are used in white papers. The illustration on the next page provides an example of how to add descriptions to a business graphic that will engage the short attention white paper reader.

1. Label the Graphic—Start the title of the graphic with the word *figure* or *illustration* along with a number, such as "Figure 1." In addition, make sure the figure is referenced in the descriptive paragraph, such as "as illustrated below in figure 1." This name/number reference system provides a placeholder that will allow the reader to quickly find the detailed descriptive information within the body copy that pertains to the graphic. It also helps organize the use of several graphics during the white paper draft stage by determining where they should be within the primary white paper pages.

2. Use a Brief Title—Make sure the chart title is no larger than the width of your business or concept graphic and certainly fits within the width of the page. This restriction will force the writer to use succinct wording to describe the image. For example, in the chart below, the title reads, "The Relationship Between Grants and Profits." As you can see, the title is short and to the point.

3. Add a Descriptive Subtitle—The subtitle, which is typically placed at the bottom of the graphic, provides the reader with the primary message associated with the graphic. It also represents the "take away" message that the reader should understand that should tie into the accompanying text on that page. In the example on the next page, the fact that losses continue to rise even though grant funding is increasing provides the primary message that the reader should understand from the chart data.

4. Add Text Boxes—Descriptive text boxes, like the ones used in the graphic above, focuses reader attention to special areas of the chart that reinforce the title and subtitle messages. The use of text boxes ensures that the most important sections of the chart will be noticed and clearly understood by the white paper reader.

An Example of a Chart with Text Boxes

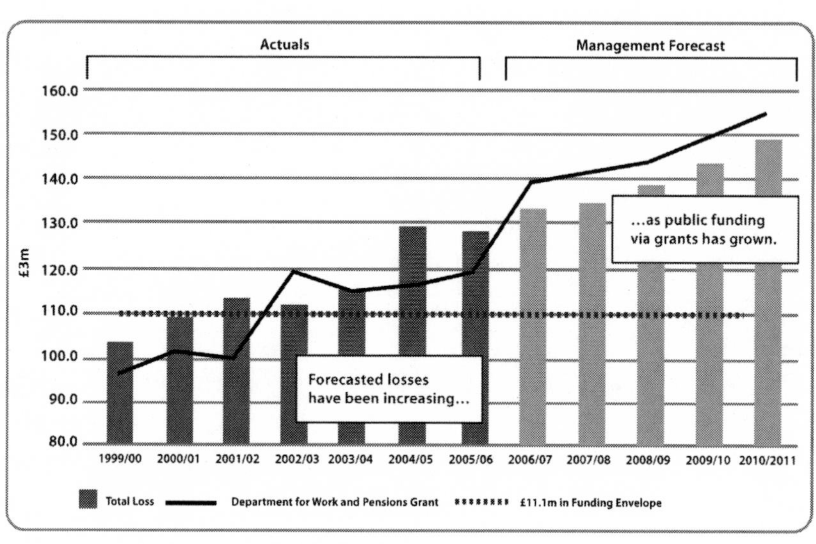

Text boxes ensure that important data trends are noticed.

5. Use a Simple Appearance—If possible, use simple charting types (column, bar, line, or pie) since they allow the reader to quickly see trends or relationships with the data without lengthy descriptive paragraphs. Complex charting types (such as scatter, radar, donut, etc.) require additional information, which defeats the quick delivery of critical messages, requiring more time, which proves ineffective for the short attention reader.

6. Include a Legend—A legend enables your reader to follow the data points in the chart and quickly comprehend associations between groups of data. The legend in the example is located at the bottom of the graphic. This allows the reader to quickly understand the difference between the data columns and the trend lines used in the chart.

7. Keep Color Choices Simple—Keep your color choices within the same color family. In the column chart above, the use of both dark and light colors of the same family shows an association between the data sets. If differences existed between the two data sets, then dramatically different color choices would be warranted. While the use of different colors can be useful to highlight an individual data point or set, using several colors within one data set or having several different data sets with separate color assignments will increase the level of visual complexity and confusion for your reader.

Chapter 15: Bullet Lists—Using Text to Gain Attention

What Are Bullets and What Is a Bullet List?

Bullets refer to the text dots, dashes, and symbols that are used to identify the various elements or items that when taken together, make up a complete concept, strategy, or plan. These individual text elements are referred to as "bulleted items."

For example, if we intended to bake a cake, we would use bullets at the beginning of each ingredient listed in the recipe. In a white paper, bullets are used to list elements, such as components of a business strategy, step-by-step procedures in a process, or suggestions that a reader can follow, to enable a suggestion advocated by the author. When bulleted items are listed, they are referred to as a "bullet list." Often, bullet lists include a bullet, followed by one or two lines of text.

There are several types of bullets that can be used in a white paper, and each one can be applied to a variety of different forms of information.

Common Bullets and a White Paper Bullet List

- The Solid Bullet
- The Open Bullet
- The Square Bullet
- The Clover-Leaf Bullet
- The Arrow Bullet
- The Checkmark Bullet

- **Partnering** - Partnering with and leveraging outsourced service providers and suppliers
- **Strategic Planning** - Mastering the tools of business planning and strategic analysis
- **Collaboration** - Driving new levels of collaboration with HR, Finance and other corporate services, business partners, and operational departments

Bullets are used to list items in a complete concept strategy.

The Solid, Open, and Square Bullets are generally the most popular types of bullets found in a white paper. These can be used with any type of listed information.

The Clover-Leaf Bullet can be applied to summary points at the end of a white paper in the concluding summary section or to add a special flair that will grab an additional level of attention to listed information.

The Arrow Bullet is common with special features when an individual item needs to be noticed within an existing list of bulleted information. For example, if we were writing a white paper about the importance of the transmission within an automotive drivetrain, we would use the arrow bullet to identify that item in a list, as follows:

The Arrow Bullet within a Bullet List

- Engine
- Differential
- Universal Joint Assembly
- Clutch

➢ **Transmission**

- Gearbox
- Axles

Arrow bullets are used to highlight a single item within a bullet list,

Finally, the **Checkmark Bullet** is used to list a sequence of items that need to be executed in a particular order, similar to a "to-do" list. In white papers, checkmark bullets are also used to list questions that the reader should ask when investigating a particular topic.

The Checkmark Bullet List

Monday's 'To-Do' List:

✓ Send Presentation to Bill
✓ Meet Chuck for Lunch
✓ Prepare Proposal for Acme Corp.
✓ Attend Planning Meeting at 4pm

Checkmark bullets are used to show a sequence of items in order.

Why Are Bullets Effective in Gaining Reader Attention?

Similar to the role of callouts in the sidebar, bullets are another effective way of gaining reader attention on a page. The unique appearance of a list of bulleted items clearly distinguishes the information they contain from other, more traditional information formats such as paragraphs. When a reader sees a list of bullets on a page, reader attention is instinctively drawn to the items on that list due to its dramatic difference from the other paragraph-oriented information. This is a great way to highlight important points that you want readers to notice given the limited amount of time and attention they can devote to reading a page with detailed information.

How Much Text Should Follow a Bullet?

For a white paper, one or two lines of information typically accompany each bullet within an overall bullet list. If the amount of information exceeds one or two lines, then the probability that the reader will read all of the information alongside that bullet diminishes significantly.

When Is Bulleted Information Considered Too Much or Ineffective?

The overuse of any single element can negatively impact the goal of quickly and effectively delivering critical information, especially for the short attention span reader. There are two things to take into consideration with bullets that may defeat the purpose of quickly delivering short business messages:

1. **Too much text**—When the information associated with a bullet becomes greater than one or two lines and approaches the size of a paragraph, then there is too much information alongside the bullet. If you find your bullets taking on the appearance of paragraphs, you need to change your formatting strategy from bullets to subheadings.

2. **Too many items**—Bullets are very effective when readers can see all of them at a glance. This usually encompasses a maximum of four or five items or elements. When the list of bulleted items exceeds this number, there is a lower likelihood that readers will be able to retain their attention throughout the entire bullet list. If a bullet list exceeds four or five elements, it may be time to reorganize that large list into smaller categories of information.

The use of bullets to draw reader attention to a list of information on a page makes it a perfect information delivery device for the time- and attention-challenged business decision maker reviewing your white paper. It should also be considered a key ingredient in your White Paper 2.0 strategy.

Chapter 16: Shaded Text Boxes—For Bottom-Line Statements

At some point in your white paper, after all problem and/or solution oriented information has been presented, it will be necessary to provide a bottom-line statement. This statement can include any of the following:

- A summary of the primary advantages associated with an identified or featured solution
- The identification of the main problem related to the white paper topic
- A conclusion reached after the presentation of all facts related to the white paper topic
- The results of a survey or poll
- A statistic that validates a situational assessment

The Shaded Text Box: Bottom-Line Statements

Between 2006 and 2008, Boomerang Tracking conducted an internal research study that examined the experiences of Boomerang subscribers.

The study calculated the total number of thefts taking place across Quebec and compared that figure to vehicles equipped with the both Boomerang Espion system (a combination of the wireless theft detection and external warning stickers) and a fleet of Boomerang protected vehicles that did not have the preventative stickers. The results show a significant advantage with the Boomerang Espion system in reducing the frequency of vehicle theft and improving the recovery rate of the stolen vehicles (See Figure 1 below).

The results showed that: The vehicles that were protected with Boomerang Espion were recovered over 90% of the time as compared with other auto theft deterrence solutions.

In addition: Vehicles that were protected with the Boomerang Espion systems were 37% less likely to be stolen, and recovered at a much faster rate if they were stolen.

A second study conducted during the same timeframe also analyzed the Sherlock Antitheft Marking System, an alternative solution that is popular with insurance providers and brokers in the region. This solution relies heavily on etching various auto parts and accessories in an effort to dissuade thieves from stealing the vehicle.

The study showed at vehicles protected with the Sherlock Antitheft Marking System **were only 27% less likely to be stolen** as compared to vehicles with no antitheft protection whatsoever, and showed an even lower likelihood that they would be recovered at all.

In addition, the vehicles protected with Boomerang Espion generated a positive return after factoring in the cost of insuring the stolen vehicles. In comparison, the vehicles protected with Boomerang Espion generated a positive return after factoring in the same coverage-related costs as compared with the Sherlock Antitheft Marking System equipped vehicles that resulted in a net loss during the same period. (see the table in Figure 2 below).

Shaded text boxes focus attention on bottom-line information.

For these and other uses, the shaded text box is the perfect formatting technique to grab reader attention and focus it on that bottom line statement. It is also an effective element in a White Paper 2.0 strategy, where attracting the short attention reader is paramount.

There are two reasons why the shaded text box is effective in grabbing reader attention and delivering important, bottom-line information:

1. **Shading**—Not only does the use of shading clearly differentiate a bottom-line statement from the primary text on the white paper page, but it also is effective with a skim reader, a person who quickly flips through the white paper pages upon initial review. Under this situation, a large shaded area will have a greater chance of being noticed

than a portion of bold or italicized text. If used appropriately, a skim reader will stop on that page and read the information contained within the shaded text box.

2. **Infrequency**—The shaded text box should only be used once or twice within a white paper. To use the shaded text box more than twice means that there is more than one single bottom-line statement. This not only leads to greater reader confusion, but it also weakens the impact of an important bottom-line message. Choose your message carefully, but stick to only one bottom-line message to generate the best results.

Does the Degree of Shading Matter?

The degree of shading for the text box doesn't matter as long as it does not get in the way of the reader's ability to read the text. If the shading is too dark, black text may be difficult to read, especially if it is printed. If you are using two shaded text boxes, make sure both use the same level of shading.

Also, a shaded text box should use the same black text as used for the rest of the text on the page. If the font is changed or its appearance is dramatically different from the primary white paper content, such as white text within a dark or black-shaded area, the visual difference may be overwhelming for the reader and may take on a "less-than-professional" appearance. This creates the same negative impression as using multiple fonts on a page. The ability to grab reader attention should be subtle and not akin to a hit on the head with a sledgehammer.

Chapter 17: White Paper Design—Natural Attraction

As readers, we are naturally attracted to photographs, illustrations, cartoons, and art. When you land on a Web site, are you are drawn to its design or to its text? In most cases, Web surfers will tout design as a primary reason to spend a greater share of their time on a particular Web site. While readers may read a large headline first, design is a critical element that draws and engages the reader to Web site content. After all, when was the last time you saw an all-text Web site, and how much time are you willing to spend there?

The same is true for a white paper. With time and attention being such a limited commodity in today's fast-paced business environment, it makes sense that a reader will naturally gravitate towards a professionally designed white paper as opposed to an all-text white paper.

To many readers who believe that a white paper should be evaluated on its text content alone, the idea of using layout and design elements to enhance the readability of a white paper flies in the face of the central premise of the medium. This viewpoint considers any use of design in a white paper along the lines of a brochure. For traditional white paper purists, this is a demeaning reference that alludes to the document as an elaborate selling medium, which is contrary to the concept of factual reporting.

Do this mean that fact-based information can't be presented in a visually pleasing format? Is the only way to present facts as cold, hard black text on a white background? Of course not. If that were the case we wouldn't see any Fortune 1000 organizations spending tens of thousands of dollars crafting professionally designed annual reports to impress their shareholders.

Just as we are attracted to a well-designed Web site, we are also attracted to a professionally designed white paper. In fact, as the use of white papers increases across many leading business industries and sectors, design will become an important, strategic attribute that will be used to distinguish one white paper from another. Certainly as the issue of attracting the short attention reader becomes more important, design will become an essential attribute used to deliver critical information to that audience. Most importantly, the use of design is an essential component within a next-generation, White Paper 2.0 marketing strategy.

Not only can design be an effective way of initially gaining reader attention, but it can also be an effective way of engaging readers, retaining reader attention, and improving the chances that a white paper will be passed along to another executive who may be part of the solution decision-making process.

What Are the Elements of a Professional White Paper Design?

1. **Text/Graphic page ratio—**On any typical white paper page, there should always be a greater amount of text than graphics. If the amount of graphics exceeds that of text, then the white paper will appear more like a brochure, harming the credibility of the content in the eyes of the business reader. It's difficult to assign a specific percentage or number to this ratio, but most readers can tell whether the graphics or the text is the most compelling aspect on a typical white paper page.

2. **Professional illustrations—**Keep in mind that the audience for white papers is typically white-collar professionals, and more than likely, executive managers and decision makers. With this group as your target audience, it is beneficial to use illustrations or images that build affinity with the professionals

reading the white paper. The illustrations should also compliment the subject.

An Example of White Paper Design

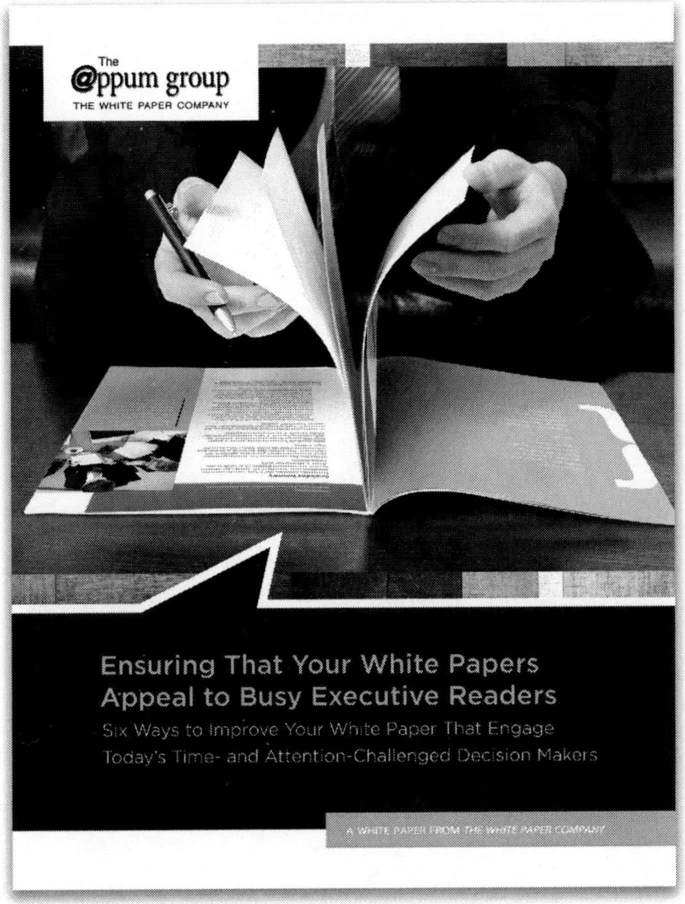

A professionally designed white paper can attract and retain reader attention.

For example, if your audience is older executives, use images of that similar age group. Conversely, if your readers are younger, more casual business professionals, then select similar images that will mimic the readers' business environment. If it is an enterprise market, use corporate images. Small business audiences should see similar images to support their work environment as well. This builds an affinity with the reader, facilitating the delivery of important business messages and solution advantages.

3. Muted Colors—Unless you need to follow specific corporate design guidelines or the look and feel of an existing set of marketing deliverables, your use of colors should be similar to the colors you would choose for your business attire. No business executive would wear a pink, electric blue, fuchsia, or yellow tie. If they did, they would not earn the respect of their executive counterparts or employees. The same strategy should hold true for the use of color in your white paper design. Muted colors such as blue, maroon, purple, green, teal, etc. work best in a business white paper. Hot colors such as red, orange, yellow, and bright versions of blue or green do not convey a professional image within the executive corridor and should be avoided. Save them for your consumer Web site and/or brochures.

4. Conservative Use of Fonts—Mixing a wide variety of different serif and san-serif fonts within the white paper pages not only creates an unprofessional look, but it also creates greater reader confusion. While it is acceptable to have different font types in your white paper, try to use the same font for each section in your white paper, such as:

- Front and rear cover titles
- Headings and subheadings
- Body copy
- Descriptions for illustrations
- Callouts/Pull quotes
- Footnotes/Endnotes

With a professional white paper design that embodies these principals, you increase the connection with your reader and improve the opportunities to deliver your most essential business/solution messages.

Chapter 18: Case Studies—Attention via Real-Life Examples

White papers are a great way to leverage educational content that is designed to convince a prospective customer to the viability of a specific solution. Unfortunately, most solution-oriented information in a white paper is theoretical, meaning that it describes how a solution is supposed to work in an ideal business situation. At some point, there is a diminishing return on page after page of theoretical solution-oriented business information.

That's where case studies come in. Case studies convince readers by showing an example of another company that might be of a similar size, in a similar industry, or experiencing similar business challenges and how the featured solution, approach, or strategy helped that company solve those particular challenges. As a result, case studies attract reader attention by increasing reader affinity and "connectivity." With this concept in mind, case studies make a valuable addition to a White Paper 2.0 strategy. After all, if the solution worked for the featured case study company, why shouldn't it also work for the reader's organization as well?

Case studies work by separating the theory of how solution advantages are *supposed* to work from the reality that shows how the solution *actually* worked in a real-life situation to solve a specific business problem.

What Is a Case Study?

Wikipedia.org defines a case study as "an intensive study of a single group, incident, or community, essentially 'a case.' Case studies include experiments, surveys, multiple histories, and analysis of archival information. They provide a systematic way of looking at events, collecting data, analyzing information, and reporting the results. As a result the researcher may gain a sharpened understanding of why the instance happened as it did, and what might become important to look at more extensively in future research."[9]

In many ways, a case study follows a similar approach to information found in a white paper. In the same way that a white paper effectively educates the reader to all aspects surrounding a topic, from industry background issues to problems assessments and finally to solution advantages, case studies apply this same orderly flow of information to a customer experience. Using this approach, a case study educates the reader to the background issues within a specific industry or marketplace that are creating the business problem, it articulates the specific business problems that are experienced by an individual company, and finally, it shows how a particular solution solved those specific problems for the organization. This approach reinforces the concept of a reality check by making a personal connection with the reader through a real-life example.

Why Integrate a Case Study into a White Paper?

Case studies have typically been viewed as a stand-alone document, in other words, as a separate and independent piece of information that does not include anything except real-life customer experiences. While case studies can certainly be used effectively in this fashion, the business marketer distributing a case study loses a strategic opportunity by not leveraging it along with solution-oriented information contained in a white paper.

A case study assumes that there is a very good match between the advocated solution in the white paper and the real-life customer situation. The solution implemented by the case study organization must be the same one described in the previous sections of the white paper. If this relationship exists, then case studies can be a highly effective way of engaging a reader by showing a proof of concept or by validating the legitimacy of the advocated solution. The connection with the reader is especially strong when the company or position presented in the case study is the same as the reader's own organizational size, circumstances, and business problem.

Anonymous Case Studies

While it would be great for every white paper to have a perfectly matched case study to accompany its solution information, the reality of these situations is completely different. Most organizations, in fact, find that having a similar one-to-one relationship is rare. In some instances, the business solution is so new that finding an organization willing to step forward and be identified in a case study is difficult. On the other hand, some customers who would make a perfect testimonial for a case study prefer not to have their company name exposed for fear that they will alert their competitors and lose a strategic business advantage within their industry.

In these situations the anonymous case study is an excellent alternative. With an anonymous case study, all of the industry dynamics, business circumstances, problems, and implementation of the solution are described as they occurred in the marketplace. The only change is that the specific name of the case study company is removed and replaced with a generic name or industry. One example of this de-identification is, "A large midwestern insurance company had a problem with its network security."

The success of the anonymous case study is largely dependent on the validity of the details used to describe the business environment and circumstances. If it accurately describes the reader's business experiences, then a very strong affinity can be build with the reader, lending in turn to a more credible case study. At this point, having an actual company name associated with the case study becomes a moot point. The accuracy of the description and how the solution solves the business problems or challenges become equally valid in the reader's eye.

What Are the Elements of a Good Case Study?

The elements of a well-written case study are similar to that of an equally well-executed white paper. Since the ideal size of an integrated white paper case study should be approximately one to two pages, the amount of information within a case study is much smaller. These elements and their relative size for an ideal case study includes:

1. **Background Introduction** (One paragraph)—Presents the environmental circumstances surrounding the customer experience. What market or industry factors contributed to the business problem the customer was experiencing?
2. **Problem Description** (One to two paragraphs)—What factors contributed to the business problem(s)? If it was the result of a competitive solution, what went wrong with that solution? If it was the result of an absence of any solution, what impact did that have on the business? A quote from an individual that experienced this problem is a valuable way to connect with the reader.
3. **Solution Assessment Process** (One paragraph)—What criteria did the case study organization execute to determine that the solution advocated in the white paper was the appropriate solution for their company? Why were other solutions not chosen?
4. **Implementation Process** (Two paragraphs)—How well was the white paper solution

implemented? Was it a smooth process, or were there difficulties that had to be overcome? A quote from an individual within the case study organization that was involved in the process is a valuable way to make a solid connection with the reader.

5. **Result After Implementation** (Two paragraphs)—What benefit(s) did the case study organization experience immediately after implementation and after six months following the implementation? Quotes are also beneficial here.

Chapter 19: Do Tables Aid the Short Attention Reader?

Like business graphics, tables are often used in white papers to show the relationship between groups of information. The difference with a table is that instead of using graphics to visualize differences between data (as with a chart), numbers and text are the only elements that are used to show the reader those differences and relationships.

The problem with tables for the short attention reader is that the information contained within their rows and columns is often difficult to fully understand by merely looking at the table alone. Often the reader needs supplemental information along with a table to fully understand the relationships between the data.

For example, in the following table, we are provided with a series of short words and phrases pertaining to the various network security threats inherent within an enterprise network environment. If we did not have any additional information except this table, would the average reader fully understand the relationship between these sets of data?

The correct answer is probably not.

In order to have the reader fully comprehend the relationship between the various sets of data in the table above, we would need several paragraphs of additional information to describe what each security threat is and why it poses an internal or external threat to an enterprise. We would also want to know what constituted a serious, malicious, or accidental threat. Real-life examples of those threats within an actual enterprise network environment would also help the reader fully understand the relationship between the tabular data.

Tables are useful in the event that paragraph-oriented text alone does not provide a concise way to adequately convey key points. For example, if we had attempted to describe the relationship between the same sets of information using only paragraphs, we would resort to an extensive use of lines and commas to articulate that same data series. After about three lines, we would lose most business readers.

Table 1: Enterprise Information Threats and Risks

TYPE OF THREAT	RISK LEVEL
External (Hacker Penetration)	
Serious "Ethical" "Just for Kicks"	Minor to Moderate Nuisance Adverse Publicity
Malicious Data Theft/Corruption/Destruction Fraud	From Minimal to Disastrous Very Serious
Internal (Improper Access)	
Accidental Breach of Confidentiality Security Loophole Created	Potentially Serious Probably Critical
Malicious Data Theft Data Corruption Fraud Data Destruction	Very Serious Very Serious Very Serious Potentially Disastrous
Denial of Service Loss of Commerce/Image	Potentially Disastrous

Tables require additional information for complete reader comprehension.

Imagine attempting to describe the information in the table above using paragraphs. Our threat assessment might look something like this:

"Enterprise security threats take on three different forms: 1) malicious threats, 2) accidental threats, and 3) serious threats, each having their own unique qualifications."

Clearly, the use of a table is helpful when there is a need to organize vast amounts of individual data sets. While the use of tables may be beneficial with certain types of white papers, unfortunately they should not be considered as a viable attention-generating element. The need to supplement the table with additional paragraphs of information may require more time and attention than most short attention readers can devote to a complex white paper page.

If you are planning to incorporate tables into your White Paper 2.0 strategy, make sure you can add additional elements described in this book so that tables won't be the only element that is employed. This will ensure that your most important business messages will be quickly noticed and remain clear for the short attention reader.

Chapter 20: A Complete White Paper 2.0 Page

The concluding summary page below was extracted from a recently completed White Paper 2.0 project. This page incorporates several attention-generating white paper elements that provide a more professional look and feel. These advanced formatting techniques lead to greater reader affinity, engagement, message retention, and a higher likelihood of reader call-to-action than a traditional all-text, paragraph-centric white paper.

A Completed White Paper 2.0 Project

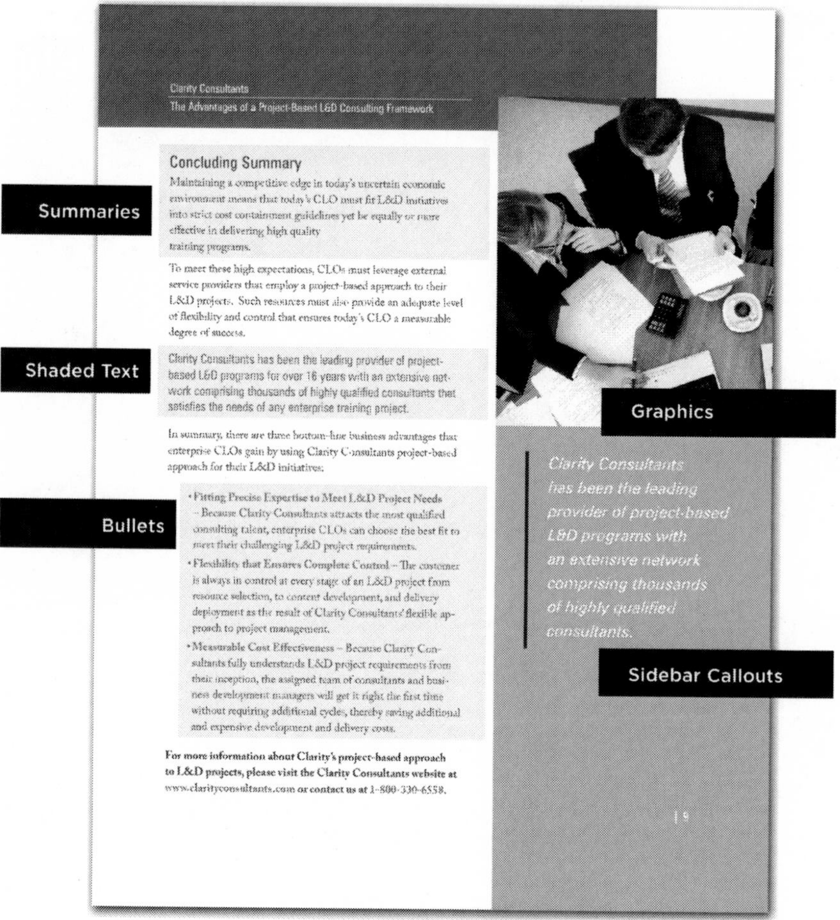

Clarity Consultants
The Advantages of a Project-Based L&D Consulting Framework

Concluding Summary

Maintaining a competitive edge in today's uncertain economic environment means that today's CLO must fit L&D initiatives into strict cost containment guidelines yet be equally or more effective in delivering high quality training programs.

To meet these high expectations, CLOs must leverage external service providers that employ a project-based approach to their L&D projects. Such resources must also provide an adequate level of flexibility and control that ensures today's CLO a measurable degree of success.

Clarity Consultants has been the leading provider of project-based L&D programs for over 16 years with an extensive network comprising thousands of highly qualified consultants that satisfies the needs of any enterprise training project.

In summary, there are three bottom-line business advantages that enterprise CLOs gain by using Clarity Consultants project-based approach for their L&D initiatives:

- Fitting Precise Expertise to Meet L&D Project Needs – Because Clarity Consultants attracts the most qualified consulting talent, enterprise CLOs can choose the best fit to meet their challenging L&D project requirements.
- Flexibility that Ensures Complete Control – The customer is always in control at every stage of an L&D project from resource selection, to content development, and delivery deployment as the result of Clarity Consultants' flexible approach to project management.
- Measurable Cost Effectiveness – Because Clarity Consultants fully understands L&D project requirements from their inception, the assigned team of consultants and business development managers will get it right the first time without requiring additional cycles, thereby saving additional and expensive development and delivery costs.

For more information about Clarity's project-based approach to L&D projects, please visit the Clarity Consultants website at www.clarityconsultants.com **or contact us at 1-800-330-6558.**

Clarity Consultants has been the leading provider of project-based L&D programs with an extensive network comprising thousands of highly qualified consultants.

| 9

Visual elements engage the short attention reader

Chapter 21: White Paper 2.0 Online Sharing and Distributing

Over the course of several chapters, we've discussed how to use a variety of visual elements in a white paper to grab the short attention business reader and deliver essential business/solution messages. But once that paper has been developed, what's next? How will you get that visually appealing white paper into the hands of the short attention reader?

As opposed to the traditional text-based white paper that was designed for hard copy printing and manual distribution, White Paper 2.0 version white papers have inherent designs that make them especially suited for online distribution across the Web.

For example, using popular tools such as Microsoft Word and Adobe Acrobat PDFs, writers can add hyperlinks and/or images into their white paper text that can direct readers to any location on the web. This capability fundamentally changes the white paper from a static text-based medium into an interactive Internet-savvy medium opening up the world of the Internet at both the writer's and the reader's disposal. As these "Web-aware" documents are distributed from person to person, department to department, or enterprise to enterprise, the ability to leverage interactive Web-based information to further influence key decision makers will increase as well.

Here is a list of the various categories of Web sites that can assist with the promotion of White Paper 2.0 documents. For a complete listing of Web sites with specific URL addresses, please visit the sections in the back of this book.

Document sharing sites—are Web sites that allow you to upload your white paper along with a description of its content. These sites require registration but do not charge a fee for uploading or downloading white papers. These sites do not provide you with e-mail or contact information for those who have downloaded your white paper.

White Paper Syndicators are Web sites that charge a fee to host your white paper and provide you with contact information for those who have reviewed and/or downloaded your white paper. Participants can use this information for sales/lead generation programs.

White Paper Blogs are Web logs focused on specific niche markets or issues that regularly update information. Users can subscribe to blogs and receive new updates via e-mail. There are several blogs specifically dedicated to the issue of white papers.

Online Forums are Web sites where interested parties can post and share comment, ideas, hyperlinks and files pertaining to white papers and other related information.

Twitter Tweets are from the social media site, Twitter, where users can send short messages of up to 140 characters in length called "Tweets" to groups of users called "followers." Hyperlinks to Web sites containing white papers are frequently attached to Twitter Tweets. Applications such as TweetDeck by Adobe allow you to setup keywords and filter the thousands of Tweet messages that contain those words. This is a good way to find white papers that others have posted or forwarded, which is referred to as "ReTweeting"(also known as RT).

Personal social media sites are sites such as Facebook, MySpace, Bebo, and Xanga are called social media sites where groups of users that share a common bond can exchange messages, files, pictures, videos, audio and other information. White papers and/or Web site links to white papers can be shared via these Web sites.

Business social media sites are sites such as LinkedIn, Plaxo, and DirectMatches.com and are similar to business-oriented Web sites designed to share common business information, leads, and sales information. White papers can be posted and shared with these sites as well.

Google Alerts allow you to setup keyword searches for white papers using the popular search engine site, Google. By setting Google Alerts to key words "white paper" or "white papers," any new listing that Google indexes containing those key words will appear each day in your e-mail inbox. These alerts will notify you of any new listing, blog post, or article that contain those key words. This is an excellent way to keep track of new white paper information posted on the web.

Chapter 22: Ten Attention-Generating Ideas for White Papers

Now that you have completed your white paper, what can you do with external resources to boost the attention for that paper?

Half the battle in getting your white paper read by a wider audience has more to do with making some simple changes that increase attention to its existence. Here are ten things you can do to gain additional exposure and attention for that white paper that will result in a higher number of downloads and greater lead generation possibilities:

1. Title It—Create a catchy title that generates interest and curiosity. Titles such as "Four Things You Need to Know About_______," or "Three Things You Didn't Know About _________" are much more compelling than "_________ Best Practices." The white paper audience likes catchy titles that create curiosity. By including titles such as these you will peak the curiosity factor of your audience and increase the chance that readers will download your white paper.

2. Cover It—Even if you have an all-text white paper, create a cover design for your document. Some suggestions for a design strategy can include similar images and colors from your Web site or other business collateral. By adding a cover, you will engage your reader and create a greater incentive to review and read it. Adding other visual elements such as pull quotes, bullets, and shaded text boxes will increase the chances that a greater portion of the document will be read by the intended audience.

3. Picture It—Thanks to the Internet, we are a more visual society. By creating a small icon of your white paper and linking that to your document, you will increase the attention and awareness of your white paper. It will also make the document easier to find than a simple text hyperlink on your Web site or blog.

4. Twitter It—Twitter is a great way to get the word out on your white paper. When you create a Tweet for your white paper, make sure you use the "shorten URL" feature to save on the number of characters used. Also only plan on using 120 characters rather than the allowed 140, so if your Tweet is ReTweeted (RT), the remaining 20 characters can accommodate additional twitter names without chopping off valuable characters for your title descriptions.

5. Sign It—Most business executives and B2B marketers send out hundreds of e-mails and correspondence every day. Add a hyperlink for your white paper below your e-mail signature. Over the course of a few months, a significant number of people will either download it, read it, or forward it to someone else they may know that has interest in the topic. This can result in a larger reading audience for your white paper that may eventually result in a larger number of warm leads over time.

6. Link It—When you add a hyperlink to your white paper using Twitter or other social media sites, make sure it directly references the URL location for the PDF. Don't link a landing page, home page, or library page that forces your reader to hunt for the link. Each additional page that you add to the process will decrease the chances that your reader *will* download or read that white paper.

7. Describe It—If you have a white paper library site that lists multiple white papers, add a brief two- or three-line description along with the title. This ensures your reader will have a better understanding of the content and if it meets their business needs. Don't force them to download and read several pages before they realize it doesn't meet their original expectations.

8. Label It—Visitors to your Web site gravitate first to the most current white papers that have been posted. Add the date the white paper was added to your Web site, and use a bright, visible "NEW" label when you post your most recent white papers so your readers will see it as soon as they land on your library page.

9. Reference It—Get others in your industry to discuss, reference, hyperlink, and forward your white paper. Sources such as Twitter, LinkedIn, industry forums, news sources, and wikis are great ways to increase exposure and the number of downloads.

10. Freely Distribute It— Give your white paper away for free without registration requirements. While the general tendency is to leverage a white paper into e-mail leads, you'll get a significantly wider reading audience (and the potential for higher leads) by giving it away without a registration requirement. Free white papers also have a higher tendency to be ReTweeted and forwarded to others.

By integrating as many of these techniques as possible into your day-to-day marketing efforts, you will dramatically increase the exposure and return on your white paper investment.

Chapter 23: Nine Attention-Robbing White Paper Mistakes

Despite many marketers' best intentions, there will always be white paper blunders that will negatively impact reader attention, especially for the short attention reader. When they happen, they deny marketers the opportunity to influence a prospective customer or target audience. Here are nine to avoid:

1. Wrong Author—Subject matter experts aren't always great communicators. A developer or user of a technology or service may know their subject inside and out, but that knowledge rarely translates to the ability to create readable, compelling prose. If your white paper is targeted to high-level business decision makers, and you want that white paper to generate results, follow this simple rule: use technical experts for input and employ a competent writer to turn your highly technical information into interesting, readable content that will be clearly understood by your business audience. This creates a positive connection that will engage the short attention reader.

2. Lack of Visual Appeal—As the book has described in length, traditional, text-heavy papers tend to lose reader attention after about three pages. When this happens, you lose your audience and your readers turn to other Web sites or solution providers for their white papers. Graphics and text treatments help get and retain reader attention. Diagrams, charts, and tables support the copy and create visual interest. Multiple columns, call-outs, and bullet lists lead the eye and enhance readability. Use visual elements to break up dense blocks of text, visually reinforce the key attributes of your solution and retain your readers' attention.

3. Acronym Abuse—The use of TLAs (three letter acronyms) and acronyms in general, such as SIP, RGB, CRM, EIM, ASP, and so on, are the bane of white paper communications. Too often, technical writers assume readers know what the acronyms mean and don't provide a clear definition or analogy to confirm how a term applies to the white paper topic. If you must use TLAs, provide clear definitions and examples. Whenever possible, use plain English instead of a TLA if you want to maintain the attention of your reader throughout your white paper.

4. Disjointed Content Flow—Too many white papers jump right into the details without providing relevant background information that explains why a business need for that solution exists in the first place. In addition, many white papers skip from one topic to another without making any connection between them. Ask yourself, "If a Martian who had just landed on earth asked what 'social media' meant, how would you describe it in detail so he could understand it?" A good white paper starts from the assumption that the reader knows nothing about the issue, presents the common business pains and problems the reader is experiencing, and highlights possible solutions to those problems. The reader is lead by a logical progression of ideas, from the problem, through possible solutions, to your solution. This logical flow retains both reader interest and attention.

5. Too Long! All too often, organizations publish white papers that cover every single point about their product or service in excruciating detail. Don't confuse your goal with that of the State Department covering the issue of famines in sub-Saharan Africa! Government white papers may need to be very long, but yours don't; a business white paper should be no more than twelve pages. Business decision makers are pressed for time and want to be able to quickly absorb the high points of your white paper. If they need more information, they will contact you. So keep it short and concise if you want it to get grab and maintain reader attention.

6. Too Short! In an effort to save time and money, many organizations will produce a short so-called white paper of two to four pages. The problem with white papers of this length is that they don't provide enough background information to bring the reader up to speed on the topic before reading about the advantages of your product or solution. A good rule of thumb is to produce your white paper with a minimum of six pages to allow enough room for discussion of the specific industry issues and business challenges your solution is designed to solve. While a short paper may retain reader attention, it may not have enough information to make an accurate assessment of your solution.

If you don't have that much material, then don't refer to the document as a white paper. Choose descriptions such as "Executive Brief" or "Corporate Perspective" to set appropriate audience expectations.

7. Audience Assumptions—Many companies fall into the trap of assuming that the target audience for their white papers already knows what the company knows about their products or solutions. This "group think" occurs when internal writers and product marketing executives deal with the same subject matter day-in and day-out. They grow accustomed to bandying about complex terms and attributes in their communications with fellow employees, vendors and support personnel who share the same level of familiarity with their solutions. When writing for an external audience, these individuals use esoteric terms and jargon that go over the heads of their readers. Remember to provide appropriate definitions, analogies and or explanations to support these complex terms for your audience if you want to retain their attention.

8. Theory without Reality—Many white papers are written as if readers will believe the effectiveness of a solution based solely on the theory of how it works. While theoretical concepts and models are essential in the educational process, they do not convey the business benefit received. Use case studies and real-world business examples that reinforce theoretical concepts to demonstrate how a particular solution can solve the specific business needs presented in your white paper. Most importantly, using real-world examples builds affinity with readers that keeps them engaged in the white paper.

9. Lack of Summaries—Have you ever read a white paper and turned the last page, only to feel as if you have just been left out in the cold? You may have presented all the facts in your white paper, but that doesn't necessarily mean that your readers have fully grasped the key points you want them to retain. The summary is your opportunity to hit the high points one last time. Think of the summary section as your chance to wrap up the white paper and ensure that the key points you wanted get across are clearly presented and understood. They also are a good way to connect with your skim readers, should they decide that the summary is the only part of the white paper that they will read.

In Summary

By avoiding these common mistakes, you can produce white papers that engage business readers, retain their attention, and most importantly, generate reader "call-to-action" that provides an appreciable return on your white paper investment.

Chapter 24: Conclusion

White papers are here to stay, and they will be a part of the business marketing landscape for some time to come. Their unique, educational, and factual approach to presenting all information surrounding an issue is very appealing in an age when readers seem to be more interested with web-based information that emphasizes the sizzle rather than the steak.

But after almost one hundred years as a text-based medium, the white paper must now evolve in order to accommodate the changing patterns of reader behavior common with today's busy business executive. As our society becomes accustomed to short, quick information messaging methods common with online media, our ability to maintain attention with lengthy and detailed text-oriented information will continue to wane. This trend will eventually place the traditional text-heavy white paper on the business endangered species list.

For today's B2B marketers, quality content must also be weighed against the readers' ability to assimilate that information. Incorporating a great writing style into a white paper that yields page after page of paragraph-oriented text may feed the writer's ego, but if that stylistic prose does not get read by its target audience, what good was the work to begin with?

As attention spans become accustomed to the Twitter model of short information delivery, traditional text white papers must now transform themselves into White Paper 2.0 models that are designed for the short attention reader.

The transition to a White Paper 2.0 strategy will build greater connectedness with the reader and improved message retention, which ultimately leads to a greater call-to-action for the white paper marketer, something that all marketers hope to achieve with their white papers.

Additional Sources for White Paper Information

There are many excellent sources of information scattered throughout the Web that will provide you with more information about white papers. These sites allow you to see white paper examples and learn how to incorporate White Paper 2.0 concepts that will make your white papers a highly effective tool within your business organization. This is a short list of Web sites that you might find especially interesting:

White Paper Blogs and Forums

1. **The White Paper Pundit Blog** (www.whitepaperpundit.com)—This is my blog, where I regularly share and discuss elements of the White Paper 2.0 concept and how to implement its strategies as part of an ongoing white paper marketing strategy.
2. **The Writing White Papers Blog** (www.writingwhitepapers.com)—Michael Stelzner's blog, where he discusses white paper trends, new studies, industry insights, and the relationship between white papers and social media marketing.
3. **The White Paper Source Online Forum** (www.whitepapersource.com)—An online forum started by Michael Stelzner, where white paper writers, marketers, users, and business professionals can share ideas, experiences, and insight related to the topic of white papers.
4. **The Click Documents Blog** (www.clickdocuments.com)—The place to find a variety of thoughts and insights on key white paper issues from

leading white paper experts. Their sister site, Click Ideas (clickideas.clickdocuments.com), also spends a considerable amount of space discussing the issue of white papers from leading contributors.

5. **The SavvyB2BMarketing Blog** (www.savvyb2bmarketing.com/blog)—This site represents a team of six diverse freelance business marketing professionals who provide a forum on issues pertaining to white papers and their role in effective business-to-business marketing
6. **The White Paper Insider Blog** (www.white-paper-insider.com/)—A blog from Apryl Parcher, Michael Stelzner's apprentice, who discusses current issues and events pertaining to white papers along with audio podcasts from leading white paper writers and authors.

White Paper Libraries and File/Document Sharing Web Sites

1. **Sribd.com** (www.scribd.com)—Scribd is a large social publishing company where millions of participants discover and share original writings and documents such as white papers. Using Scribd's iPaper document reader, anyone can easily upload and immediately share original works on Scribd.com or any other Web site. iPaper transforms print file types like PDF, Word, or PowerPoint into Web documents—retaining all the fonts, layout, and artwork of each document. Scribd's documents are indexed for search engine optimization, allowing them to be easily discovered across the world.
2. **Docstoc.com** (www.docstoc.com)—Docstoc.com is an online community designed to find and share professional documents such as white papers. Docstoc.com serves as a vast repository of documents in a variety of categories including legal, business, financial, technology,

educational, and creative. All documents on Docstoc.com can be easily searched, previewed, and downloaded for free.

3. **Issuu.com** (www.issuu.com)—Issuu.com is a free Web site that allows marketers to post a variety of documents, publications, and white papers and publish them to an audience of millions of prospective readers. The site allows subscribers to create a custom viewer design and integrate your publications on your Web site.
4. **SlideShare.net** (www.slideshare.net)—SlideShare.net is the world's largest community for sharing presentations. Users can also upload documents such as white papers or find white papers on topics that interest them. They can tag, download, or embed white papers into their own blogs and Web sites.
5. **Gazhoo.com** (www.gazhoo.com)—Gazhoo.com bills itself as the content marketplace. It is, in effect, a place where anyone can sell their intellectual goods in the form of documents such as white papers. Fortunately, each document can be previewed prior to purchase, so you can evaluate it before purchasing.
6. **Yudu.com (**www.yudu.com)—Yudu.com is a free library of digital content to read and explore. You can find eBooks, magazines, and white papers, as well as photos, music, podcasts, and bookmarks and add them to your own library. You can create your own interest groups and join other people's to share your passions, experiences, and knowledge with like-minded users.

White Paper Syndicators and Vertical White Paper Web Sites

1. **Bitpipe.com** (www.bitpipe.com)**—**Bitpipe.com is an online network of information technology (IT) and business Web sites that pioneered the concept of creating

multiple distribution channels for vendor-created content such as white papers. It is one of the leading resources for enterprise information technology. Bitpipe's comprehensive suite of services enable information-technology marketers to syndicate their white papers, product information, Webcasts, case studies, and analyst reports through the Bitpipe network of IT and business-related partner sites, including Bitpipe.com, BusinessWeek, Google, and other leading IT and business-related destinations.

2. **TechTarget.com** (www.techtarget.com)—TechTarget publishes integrated media that enable technology providers to reach targeted communities of technology professionals and executives in all phases of their decision-making and purchase processes. A significant part of TechTarget's content includes white papers from many leading enterprise solution providers across several industries. TechTarget also includes a sister site, KnowledgeStorm.com, which contains another popular online white paper library and resource.
3. **TechRepublic.com** (whitepapers.techrepublic.com.com)—TechRepublic is one of the largest libraries of vendor-supplied technical content on the Web, including white papers. TechRepublic.com has two additional white paper library sites located on **ZDNet.com** (www.zdnet.com) and on **BNET.com** (www.bnet.com).
4. **BankInfoSecurity.com** (www.bankinfosecurity.com)—This site is an information portal that includes white papers on the topic of banking, credit unions, and other financially related enterprises. Their companion site, **CUInfoSecurity.com**, (www.cuinfosecurity.com) offers similar information for credit unions.

5. **Techweb.com** (www.techweb.com)—Techweb.com is a leading technology information resource that includes white papers. Techweb.com online brands include InformationWeek, Interop, VoiceCon, Light Reading, Dark Reading, Black Hat, and Web 2.0 Summit. The site has more than 13.3 million business technology professional subscribers that include CIOs, senior-level IT managers, developers, communications service providers, and business executives from small and mid-sized organizations to global enterprises across all vertical industries.
6. **FindWhitePapers.com** (www.findwhitepapers.com)—Find White Papers is an industry-leading research and white paper library, which serves as a source of knowledge and information for the technology and business professional alike. With topics ranging from Wireless Security, Business Intelligence Software, Enterprise Resource Planning, and more than three hundred additional areas, Find White Papers is one of the largest repositories of information technology intelligence found on the Internet.
7. **IndustryWeek.com** www.industryweek.com)—Industry Week.com is a leading online information resource supporting manufacturers and the manufacturing industry. The site includes a well-stocked library of manufacturing white papers on business issues, strategies, trends, and technologies, which are all posted as PDFs.
8. **ITBusinessEdge.com** (www.itbusinessedge.com)—IT Business Edge is an IT information portal that incorporates powerful search technologies to improve the retrieval of business information and white papers. This unique approach delivers information that is focused, personalized, thorough, practical, concise, and current. Its timely and pertinent information provides top-level IT decision makers with the ability to keep track of technical advances and new solutions

and to pursue IT strategies that are most appropriate for their organizations.

9. **Toolbox.com** (www.toolbox.com)—Toolbox.com is a network of online communities for IT, human resources, and finance that includes an extensive white paper library for each of these sectors. Through Toolbox.com, executives and professionals can collaborate with their peers to resolve problems more efficiently, make better decisions by leveraging best practices and lessons learned, and increase their efficiency in the workplace.
10. **TradePub.com** (www.tradepub.com)—TradePub.com is a sophisticated repository of several different types of online content, including white papers for business professionals in over thirty-three industry verticals, with extensive reach through thousands of B2B partner sites worldwide.
11. **RetailWire.com** (www.retailwire.com)—RetailWire.com is the retailing industry's premier online discussion forum, which includes an extensive library of white papers on retail industry issues. Over two-thirds of RetailWire.com members are in top executive or senior management positions, representing a broad cross-section of retail channels and the companies that supply them. RetailWire.com is supported via sponsorships by leading retail suppliers and service organizations.
12. **WebBuyersGuide.com** (www.webbuyersguide.com)—The Web Buyer's Guide (WBG) is the industry's leading online technology directory designed to support enterprise IT buyers and decision makers by supplying them with the right mix of comprehensive and informative content they need to make educated purchasing decisions. Organized by over one thousand product categories and nearly nine hundred content topics, the WBG provides buyers with immediate access to all the critical information used in the technology-

buying process, including Ziff Davis Enterprise editorial and vendor content such as white papers, Webcasts, case studies, research reports, videos, and podcasts.

13. **Whitepapers.org** (www.whitepapers.org)—
Whitepapers.org is a fee-free white paper sharing site where marketers across several industries can upload and promote their white papers. Featured categories include technology and business areas such as finance, human resources, marketing, and sales. Featured industries include banking, consumer products, government, healthcare, manufacturing, retail, telecommunications, and many others.

About Jonathan Kantor

Jonathan Kantor is the principal and founder of The Appum Group: "The White Paper Company," a technical marketing organization that specializes in the creation of professional business and technical white papers for enterprise-class, medium, and small organizations.

Prior to the formulation of The Appum Group, Jonathan was the senior technical communications manager for J.D. Edwards Enterprise Software ($1.7 Billion), which has since been acquired by Oracle Corporation. In this former capacity, Jonathan directed a team of technical marketing and graphics professionals responsible for the development of the J.D. Edwards corporate white paper strategy, which was a critical part of their external technical communication process.

Jonathan's experience with white papers is also coupled with over twenty-six years of business experience with leading technology innovators including Apple Computer, Microsoft, and Digital Equipment Corporation, where he held a variety of sales, marketing, business development, and management positions.

Since its founding in 2000, Appum Group customers have included a significant number of enterprise small to medium businesses across many different industries, including technology, finance, insurance, construction, human resources, non-profits, pharmaceutical, and consulting services.

Jonathan is also the author of the White Paper Pundit blog, at www.whitepaperpundit.com. To contact Jonathan, please send an e-mail to info@appum.com or via Twitter at Jonathan_Kantor.

Notes

1. "The 2008 B2B Technology Collateral Survey," Eccolo Media, November 2008.

2. "White Paper Case Study 2007," Arbor Networks, March 2007.

3. "A Day in the Life of C-Level Executives, Part VIII," Forbes.com and GartnerG2, January 2008.

4. "The Sum of Social Media—Is It All Just Hype?" InHouse Assist LLC, http://bit.ly/vOvQB, page 2.

5. Definition of the term *social media*, Wikipedia.org, http://en.wikipedia.org/wiki/Social_media.

6. "Long vs. Short Articles as Content Strategy," Jakob Nielsen's Alertbox, Useit.com, http://www.useit.com/alertbox/content-strategy.html, November 12, 2007.

7. "How to Maximize the Use of White Papers in Your B2B Marketing and Sales Process," InformationWeek Business Technology Network.

8. "How to Maximize the Use of White Papers in Your B2B Marketing and Sales Process," InformationWeek.com, February 2009, references slide 25.

9. Definition of the term *case study*, Wikipedia.org: http://en.wikipedia.org/wiki/Case_study.

Index